THE PHILOSOPHER AND THE WOLF

Lessons from the Wild on Love, Death and Happiness

Mark Rowlands

GRANTA

Granta Publications, 12 Addison Avenue, London W11 4QR

First published in Great Britain by Granta Books, 2008
This paperback edition published by Granta Books, 2009

A CIP catalogue record for this book
is available from the British Library.

7 9 10 8 6

ISBN 978 1 84708 102 5

Printed in the UK by CPI Bookmarque, Croydon, CR0 4TD

For Emma

Contents

Acknowledgements

George Miller first commissioned this book for Granta. This was almost certainly an act of great faith on George's part since, by common consensus, no one really had a clue what was going on in the early drafts of the book. When George left, the editorial process was taken over by Sara Holloway, who is a dream of an editor. Her perceptive, intelligent and, above all, patient questions, and her determination to make sure that I didn't lose track of what was important, made this book much better than it would otherwise have been. The copy-editing was done by Lesley Levene. Never, in my fairly extensive experience, has the copy-editing process been so painless, even faintly enjoyable, and never have I learned so much about the art of writing from this process. My deepest thanks to all three parties. Thanks also to Vicki Harris for consistently excellent proof-reading. And thanks, it goes without saying, to my agent, Liz Puttick, for getting yet another one of my crazy projects off the ground.

This book would not exist without its subject matter. So, thank you, Brenin, my wolf brother, for sharing your life with me – and, of course, thanks to your sidekicks Nina and Tess.

Finally, to Brenin: my son and not my brother. I can't say that I wrote this book for you, because it was begun before you were even a glint in your old man's eye. But I finished it because I wanted you to understand your name. That and I had spent the advance. Remember, in the end, and how many times I am going to regret saying this I shudder to think: it is only our defiance that redeems us.

Mark Rowlands
Miami

1

The Clearing

1

This is a book about a wolf called Brenin. For more than a decade – during most of the 1990s and some of the 2000s – he lived with me. As a consequence of sharing the life of a rootless and restless intellectual, he became an extraordinarily well-travelled wolf, living in the US, Ireland, England and, finally, France. He was also the, largely unwilling, beneficiary of more free university education than any wolf that ever lived. As you will see, dire consequences would ensue for my house and possessions should I leave him unattended. So I had to bring him into work with me – and as I was a philosophy professor, this meant bringing him to my lectures. He would lie in the corner of the room and doze – much like my students really – while I droned on about some or other philosopher or philosophy. Occasionally, when the lectures became particularly tedious, he would sit up and howl – a habit that endeared him to the students, who had probably been wishing they could do the same thing.

This is also a book about what it means to be human – not as a biological entity but as a creature that can do things no other creatures can. In the stories we tell about ourselves, our uniqueness is a common refrain. According to some, this lies in our ability to create civilization, and so protect ourselves from nature, red in tooth and claw. Others point to the fact that we are the only creatures that can understand the difference between good and evil, and therefore are the only creatures truly capable of being good or evil. Some say we are unique because we have reason; we are rational animals alone in a world of irrational brutes. Others think it is our use of language that decisively separates us from dumb animals. Some say we are unique because we alone are capable of free will and action. Others think our uniqueness lies in the fact that we alone are capable of love. Some say that we alone are capable of understanding the nature and basis of true happiness. Others think we are unique because we alone can understand that we are going to die.

I don't believe any of these stories as accounts of a critical gulf between us and other creatures. Some of the things we think they can't do, they can. And some of the things we think we can do, we can't. As for the rest, well, it's mostly a matter of degree rather than kind. Instead, our uniqueness lies simply in the fact that we tell these stories – and, what's more, we can actually get ourselves to believe them. If I wanted a one-sentence definition of human beings, this would do: humans are the animals that believe the stories they tell about themselves. Humans are credulous animals.

In these dark times, it does not need emphasizing that the stories we tell about ourselves can be the biggest source of division between one human and another. From credulity, there is often but a short step to hostility. However, I am concerned with the stories we tell to distinguish ourselves not from each other but from other animals: the stories we tell about what makes us human. Each story has what we might call a dark side; it casts a shadow. That shadow is to be found behind what the story says; here you will find what the story shows. And this is likely to be dark in at least two ways. First of all, what the story shows is often a deeply unflattering, even disturbing, facet of human nature. Second, what the story shows is often difficult to see. The two senses are not unconnected. We humans have a pronounced facility for passing over the aspects of ourselves we find distasteful. And this extends to the stories we tell to explain ourselves to ourselves.

The wolf is, of course, the traditional, if unfairly selected, representative of the dark side of humanity. This is in many ways ironic — not least etymologically. The Greek word for wolf is *lukos*, which is so close to the word for light, *leukos*, that the two were often associated. It may be that this association was simply the result of mistakes in translation, or it may be that there was a deeper etymological connection between the two words. But for whatever reason Apollo was regarded as both the god of the sun and the god of wolves. And in this book it is the connection between the wolf and the light that is important. Think of the wolf as the clearing in the forest. In the bowels of the forest, it may be too dark to see the trees. The clearing is the place that allows what was hidden to be uncovered. The wolf, I shall try to show, is the clearing in the human soul. The wolf uncovers what is hidden in the stories we tell about ourselves — what those stories show but do not say.

We stand in the shadow of the wolf. Something can cast a shadow in two ways: by occluding light or by being the source of light that other things occlude. We talk of the shadows cast by a man and those cast by a fire. By the shadow of the wolf, I mean not the shadow cast by the wolf itself, but the shadows we cast from the light of the wolf. And staring back at us from these shadows is precisely what we don't want to know about ourselves.

2

Brenin died a few years ago. I still find myself thinking about him every day. This may strike many as overly indulgent: he was, after all, just an animal. Nonetheless, despite my life now being, in all important respects, the best it's ever been, I have become, I think, a diminished thing. It's really hard to explain why, and for a long time I didn't understand. Now I think I do — Brenin taught me something that my protracted formal education did not and could not teach me. And it's a lesson that is difficult to retain, with the necessary level of clarity and vibrancy, now that he has gone. Time heals, but it does so through erasure. This book is an attempt to record the lesson before it is gone.

There is an Iroquois myth that describes a choice the nation was once forced to make. The myth has various forms. This is the simplest version. A council of the tribes was called to decide where to move on for the next hunting season. What the council had not known, however, was that the place they eventually chose was a place inhabited by wolves. Accordingly, the Iroquois became subject to repeated attacks, during which the wolves gradually whittled down their numbers. They were faced with a choice: to move somewhere else or to kill the wolves. The latter option, they realized, would diminish them. It would make them the sort of people they did not want to be. And so they moved on. To avoid repetition of their earlier mistake, they decided that in all future council meetings someone should be appointed to represent the wolf. Their contribution would be invited with the question, 'Who speaks for wolf?'

This is the Iroquois version of the myth, of course. If there were a wolf version, I am sure it would be quite different. Nonetheless, there is truth here. I am going to try and show you that, for the most part, each one of us has the soul of an ape. I'm not investing too much in the word 'soul'. By 'soul' I don't necessarily mean some immortal and incorruptible part of us that survives the death of our bodies. The soul may be like this, but I doubt it. Or it may be that the soul is simply the mind, and the mind is simply the brain. But, again, I doubt it. As I am using the word, the soul of human beings is revealed in the stories they tell about themselves: stories about why they are unique; stories we humans can actually get ourselves to believe, in spite of all the evidence against them. These, I am going to argue, are stories told by apes: they have a structure, theme and content that is recognizably simian.

I am, here, using the ape as a metaphor for a tendency that exists, to a greater or lesser extent, in all of us. In this sense, some humans are more apes than others. Indeed, some apes are more apes than others. The 'ape' is the tendency to understand the world in instrumental terms: the value of everything is a function of what it can do for the ape. The ape is the tendency to see life as a process of gauging probabilities and computing possibilities, and using the results of these computations in its favour. It is the tendency to see the world as a collection of resources; things to be used for its purposes. The ape applies this principle to other apes as much as, or even more than, to the rest of the natural world. The ape is the tendency to have not friends, but allies. The ape does not see its fellow apes; it watches them. And all the while it waits for the opportunity to take advantage. To be alive, for the ape, is to be waiting to strike. The ape is the tendency to base relationships with others on a single principle, invariant and unyielding: what can you do for me, and how much will it cost me to get you to do it? Inevitably, this understanding of other apes will turn back on itself, infecting and informing the ape's view of itself. And so it thinks of its happiness as something that can be measured, weighed, quantified and calculated. It thinks of love in the same way. The ape is the tendency to think that the most important things in life are a matter of cost-benefit analysis.

This, I should reiterate, is a metaphor that I use to describe a human tendency. We all know people like this. We meet them at work and at play; we have sat across conference tables and restaurant tables from them. But these people are just exaggerations of the basic human type. Most of us, I suspect, are more like it than we realize or would care to admit. But why do I describe this tendency as simian? Humans are not the only sorts of apes that can suffer and enjoy the gamut of human emotions. As we shall see, other apes can feel love; they can feel grief so intense that they die from it. They can have friends, and not just allies. Nevertheless, this tendency is simian in the sense that it is made possible by apes; more pre- cisely, by a certain sort of cognitive development that took place in the apes and, as far as we know, no other animal. The tendency to see the world and those in it in cost-benefit terms; to think of one's life, and the important things that happen in it, as things that can be quantified and calculated: this ten- dency is possible only because there are apes. And of all the apes, this tendency receives its most complete expression in us. But there is also a part of our soul that existed long before we became apes – before this tendency could catch us in its grip – and this is hidden in the stories we tell about ourselves. It is hidden, but it can be uncovered.

Evolution works by gradual accretion. In evolution, there is no *tabula rasa*, no clean slate: it can work only with what it is given and never go back to the drawing board. Thus, to use the stock example, the grotesquely twisted features of the flat fish – one of whose eyes has in essence been pulled around the other side – are evidence that the evolutionary pressures that led a fish to specialize in lying on the sea bed were pressures acting on a fish that had originally developed for other purposes and, therefore, had eyes located on its lateral, rather than dorsal, surfaces. Similarly, in the development of human beings, evolution was forced to work with what it was given. Our brains are essentially historical structures: it is on the foundations of a primitive limbic system – one that we share with our reptilian ancestors – that the mammalian cortex – the particularly brawny version of which is characteristic of human beings – has been built.

I don't mean to suggest that the stories we tell, and believe, about ourselves are evolutionary products like the flat fish's eyes or the mammalian brain. However, I do think that they are built in a similar way: through gradual accretion, where new layers of narrative are superimposed on older structures and themes. There is no clean slate for the stories we tell about ourselves. I shall try to show that if we look hard enough, and if we know where and how to look, then in every story told by apes we shall also find a wolf. And the wolf tells us – this is its function in the story – that the values of the ape are crass and worthless. It tells us that what is most important in life is never a matter of calculation. It reminds us that what is of real value cannot be quantified or traded. It reminds us that sometimes we must do what is right though the heavens fall.

We are, all of us I think, more ape than wolf. In many of us, the wolf has been almost completely expunged from the narrative of our lives. But it is at our peril that we allow the wolf to die. In the end the ape's schemes will come to nothing; its cleverness will betray you and its simian luck will run out. Then you will find what is most important in life. And this is not what your schemes and cleverness and luck have bought you; it is what remains when they have deserted you. You are many things. But the most important you is not the one who schemes; it is the one who remains when the scheming fails. The most important you is not the one who delights in your cunning; it is what is left behind when this cunning leaves you for dead. The most important you is not the one who rides your luck; it is the you who remains when that luck has run out. In the end, the ape will always fail you. The most important question you can ask yourself is: when this happens, who is it that will be left behind?

It took a long time, but at last I think I understand why I loved Brenin so much, and miss him so painfully now he has gone. He taught me something that my extended formal education could not: that in some ancient part of my soul there still lived a wolf.

Sometimes it is necessary to let the wolf in us speak; to silence the incessant chattering of the ape. This book is an attempt to speak for wolf in the only way that I can.

3

'The only way that I can' turned out quite differently from what I had planned. This book took me a long time to write.

In one way or another, I've been working on it for the best part of fifteen years. This is because the thoughts that it contains took me a long time to think. Sometimes, wheels turn slowly. The book grew out of my life with a wolf, but there is, I think, still a very real sense in which I don't understand what this book is.

It is, in one sense, autobiographical. All the events described here happened. They happened to me. But there are also so many ways in which it is not an autobiography; at least not a good one. If there is a star of the book, of course, then it's not me. I'm just an insignificant extra bumbling around in the background. Good autobiographies are richly populated with other people. But in this book other people figure mainly by way of their absence – you may find the ghosts of the other people in my life, but that is all. To protect the privacy of these ghosts, since I have no idea whether they would be enthusiastic about appearing, I have changed their names. And when there are other things I wish to protect, I find myself being coy with details of location or timeline. Good autobiographies are also detailed and comprehensive. Here, however, the details are sparse and the memory is selective. The book is driven by what I learned from my life with Brenin, and I have organized it around these lessons. To this end, I have focused largely on those events in the life of Brenin and myself that are pertinent to the thoughts that I wanted to develop. Other episodes, some of them significant, have been ignored and will soon be lost in time. When specific details of events, persons or chronology threatened to overwhelm the thoughts I wanted to develop, I ruthlessly excised them.

If this did not turn out to be the story of me, then neither did it really end up being the story of Brenin. Of course, the book is built around various events that occurred during our life together. But it is only rarely that I try to understand what is going on in his mind during those events. Despite living with him for more than a decade, I'm not sure I'm competent to make such judgements in anything but the most simple of cases. And many of the events I describe and the issues I discuss through them are not simple. Brenin figures – I believe strongly – in this book as a concrete, brooding presence. But he also appears in a quite different way: as a symbol or metaphor for an aspect of me, an aspect that, perhaps, is no more. Thus I find myself sometimes lapsing into metaphorical talk of what the wolf 'knows'. If this were taken as an empirical speculation about the actual content of Brenin's mind, these claims would be risibly anthropomorphic. But, I assure you, they are not intended to function in this way. Similarly, when I talk of the lessons I learned from Brenin, these were visceral and fundamentally non-cognitive. They were learned not from studying Brenin, but from the fact that the paths of our lives were walked together. And many of the lessons I did not understand until after he was gone.

Nor is this a work of philosophy, at least not in the narrow sense in which I have been trained and of which my professional colleagues would approve. There are arguments. But there is no neat progression from premises to conclusion. Life is too slippery for premises and conclusions. Instead, I'm struck by the overlapping character of the discussions of this book. I'm struck by how an issue that I had intended to deal with and put to bed in one chapter can insist on reasserting itself later on, in a new, mutated form. This, it seems, is a consequence of the nature of the investigation. Life rarely allows itself to be dealt with and put to bed.

The thoughts that drive this book are ones I have thought but, nevertheless, in an important sense, are not mine. This is not because they are someone else's – although one can clearly discern the influence of thinkers such as Nietzsche, Heidegger, Camus, Kundera and the late Richard Taylor. Rather, and once again I must resort to metaphor, I think there are certain thoughts that can emerge only in the space between a wolf and a man.

In our early days, Brenin and I used to take off some weekends to Little River Canyon in the north-eastern corner of Alabama and (illegally) pitch a tent. We'd spend the time chilling and howling at the moon. The canyon was narrow and deep, and it was with reluctance that the sun would push its way through the dense druid oaks and birches. And once the sun had passed over the western rim, the shadows would congeal into a solid bank. After an hour or so of easing ourselves along a neglected trail, we would enter the clearing. If we had timed things just right, it would be as the sun gave its parting kiss to the canyon's lip, and golden light would reverberate through the open space. Then the trees, largely hidden by the gloom for the past hour, would stand out in their aged and mighty splendour. The clearing is the space that allows the trees to emerge from the darkness into the light. The thoughts that make up this book emerged in a space that no longer exists, and would not have been possible – at least not for me – without that space.

The wolf is no more and therefore the space is no more. When I read through what I have written, I am struck by just how alien are the thoughts it contains. That I was the one to think them strikes me as a strange discovery. These are not my thoughts because, while I believe them and hold them to be true, I would not be capable of thinking them again. These are the thoughts of the clearing. These are thoughts that exist in the space between a wolf and a man.

2

Brotherwolf

1

Brenin never lay down in the back of the Jeep. He always liked to see what was coming. Once, many years ago, we had driven from Tuscaloosa, Alabama, all the way down to Miami – around 800 miles – and back again. And he stood every inch of the way: his hulking presence blocking out much of the sun and all of the rear traffic. But this time, on this short drive into Béziers, he wouldn't stand; couldn't stand. And it was then I knew he was gone. I was taking him to the place where he would die. I had told myself that if he stood up, even for part of the journey, I would give it another day; another twenty-four hours for a miracle to occur. But now I knew it was it over. My friend of the past eleven years would be gone. And I didn't know what sort of person he was going to leave behind.

The dark French midwinter could not have contrasted

more starkly with that bright Alabama evening, in early May, a little over a decade earlier, when I first brought six-week-old Brenin into my house and into my world. Within two minutes of his arrival – and I am by no means exaggerating – he had pulled the curtains in the living room (both sets!) off their rails and on to the ground. Next, while I was trying to rehang the curtains, he found his way out into the garden and under the house. At the rear, the house was raised off the ground and you could access the area underneath by way of a door built into the brick wall – a door that I had obviously left ajar.

He made his way under the house and then proceeded – methodically, meticulously but above all quickly – to rip down every single one of the soft, lagged pipes that directed the cold air from the air-conditioning unit up through various vents in the floor. That was Brenin's trademark attitude to the new and unfamiliar. He liked to see what was coming. He would explore it; embrace it. Then he would trash it. He was mine for all of an hour and already he had cost me $1,000 – $500 to buy him and $500 to repair the air conditioning. And in those days that was not far off one-twentieth of my gross annual salary. This sort of pattern would repeat itself, in often quite innovative and imaginative ways, through all the years of our association. Wolves do not come cheap.

So, if you were thinking of acquiring a wolf, or wolf–dog mix for that matter, the first thing I would say to you is: don't do it! Don't ever do it; don't even think about it. They are not dogs. But if you foolishly persist, then I would tell you that your life is about to change for ever.

2

I was a couple of years into my first job – Assistant Professor of Philosophy at the University of Alabama, in a city called Tuscaloosa. 'Tuscaloosa' is a Choctaw word that means 'Black Warrior', and the huge Black Warrior River flows through it. Tuscaloosa is best known for its university's (American) football team, the Crimson Tide, which the local community embraces with a fervour that surpasses the merely religious – although they're heavily into that too. I think it's fair to say that they're far more suspicious of philosophy – and who can blame them. Life was good; I had far too much fun in Tuscaloosa. But I had grown up with dogs – mostly big dogs like Great Danes – and I missed them. And so, one afternoon, I found myself looking through the want-ads section of the *Tuscaloosa News*.

For much of its relatively short life, the United States of America pursued a policy of systematic eradication of its wolves – through shooting, poisoning, trapping, whatever means necessary. The result is that there are virtually no free wild wolves in the contiguous forty-eight states. Now that the policy has been abandoned, they've started to make a comeback in parts of Wyoming, Montana and Minnesota, and on some of the islands in the Great Lakes – Isle Royale, off the northern coast of Michigan, being the most famous example, largely due to some groundbreaking research on wolves conducted there by the naturalist David Mech. They have even recently been reintroduced, over the strident protestations of ranchers, into the most famous of US natural parks, Yellowstone.

This resurgence in the wolf population, however, has not yet reached Alabama or the South in general. There are lots of coyotes. And there are a few red wolves, in the swamps of Louisiana and east Texas – though no one is really sure what they are, and they may well be the result of historical wolf–coyote hybridization. But timber wolves, or grey wolves as they are sometimes known (inaccurately – since they can also be black, white and brown), are a distant memory in the Southern states.

Therefore I was somewhat surprised when my eye was caught by an advertisement: wolf cubs for sale, 96 per cent. After a quick phone call, I jumped in the car and headed off to Birmingham, about an hour to the north-east, not entirely sure what I was expecting to find. And so it was, a little later, that I came to be standing, eyeball to eyeball, with the biggest wolf I had ever heard of, let alone seen. The owner had shown me around to the back of the house, and the stable and pen that housed the animals. When the father wolf – who was called Yukon – heard us coming he jumped up at the stable door, just as we arrived there, appearing as if from nowhere.

He was huge and imposing, standing slightly taller than me. I had to look up at his face and his strange yellow eyes. But it was his feet I will always remember. People don't real-ize – certainly I didn't – just how big wolves' feet are, much bigger than those of dogs. It was his feet that announced Yukon's arrival, the first things I saw as he bounded up to lean over the stable door. They now hung over that door, much bigger than my fists, like furry baseball mitts.

One thing people often ask me, not about this situation in particular – because this is the first time I've told anyone of it – but about owning a wolf in general: aren't you ever scared of him? The answer is, of course, no. I would like to think that this is because I'm an inordinately brave person, but that hypothesis would fly in the face of a large body of counter-vailing evidence. I need several stiff drinks before I'll even set foot on a plane, for example. So, unfortunately, I don't think the attribution of any general-purpose bravery can be sustained. But I am very relaxed around dogs. And this is largely the result of my upbringing: I am the dysfunctional product of a rather dysfunctional family. Happily this dysfunction was – as far as I'm aware – restricted to our interactions with dogs.

When I was young, around two or three, we used to play a game with Boots, our Labrador. He would lie down, and I would sit on his back and hold on to his collar. Then my father would call him. Boots, lightning fast in his younger days, would be on his feet and running in a fraction of a second. My job – the aim of the game – was to hold on to his collar and ride on his back. I never could. It was like I was a dining set and someone pulled the tablecloth out from under me. Sometimes the canine magician's technique was spot on and I would be left sitting on the ground, in the place where Boots had been lying the moment before, looking somewhat puzzled. Sometimes, however, Boots would get a little sloppy and I would tumble head over heels to the ground. But in this game, any pain would be treated as the minor irrelevance that it was and I would spring up from the grass in glee, begging for a chance to try again. You probably couldn't get away with this today in our chronically risk-averse culture, with its neurotic attitude towards the possibility of broken bones in the young. Someone would probably call child services, or maybe animal services – or possibly both. But I know I cursed the day when my father told me I had grown too big and heavy to play this game with Boots any more.

Looking back on things, I realize that, when it comes to dogs, my family, and consequently I, are just not normal. We would often take in Great Danes from rescue centres. Sometimes these were lovely animals. Sometimes they were positively psychotic. Blue, a Great Dane unimaginatively named – not by us – after his colour, provides a good case in point. Blue was about three years old when my parents rescued him. And it was easy to understand why he found himself in a rescue centre. Blue had a hobby: the random and indiscriminate biting of people and other animals. Actually, that's not fair: it wasn't random or indiscriminate at all. He just had various, let us call them, idiosyncrasies. One of them was not permitting people to leave the room when he was in it. You could never afford to find yourself in a room with Blue on your own. You always needed someone to distract him while you exited. Of course, they would then need someone else to distract Blue should they wish to leave the room. And so the great wheel of Blue's life turned. Failure to adequately distract him before exiting the room would often result in one's hindquarters being scarred for life. Just ask my brother, Jon.

My family's abnormality exhibited itself not just in their willingness to accept Blue's idiosyncrasies – instead of sending him on a one-way ticket to the vet, like any normal family would have done. More than that, it was in the way they regarded this rather disturbing facet of Blue's personality as a source of enormous mirth: indeed, as a rather enjoyable game. Most people would probably think, correctly, that Blue was a recidivist danger to limb and possibly life and that, all things considered, the world might be better off without him. But my family enjoyed the game. I think all of them bear the scars of Blue's idiosyncrasies – and not just on their hindquarters: Blue had other idiosyncrasies too. I alone escaped, but that's because I had left home for university by the time he arrived on the scene. However, the scars were seen not as sources of sympathy or concern, but as opportunities for general ribbing and gentle ridicule.

Insanity, of course, runs in families; and it was, perhaps, too much to expect me to escape it. A few years ago I found myself playing a daily game with a Dogo Argentino that lived near me in a village in France. These are large, powerful white dogs, like oversized versions of pit bulls, and have been banned in the UK under the Dangerous Dogs Act. When she was a puppy, whenever she saw me, she would excitedly charge up to her garden fence and jump up for me to pat her. As she grew older she continued this behaviour. But at a certain point she obviously decided that, all things considered, it might be a good idea to bite me too. Happily for me, while Dogos are big and strong dogs, they are not fast. Nor are they particularly intelligent: I could almost see the wheels turning in her head while she pondered the possibilities and consequences of biting me. And so each day we would play the same game. I walked past; she would jump up at the fence; I would pat her head; she would enjoy the patting for a few seconds, snuffling her nose into my hand with her tail wagging away merrily; but then her body would stiffen and her mouth purse. Then she would snap at me. To be fair, I think it was pretty half-hearted stuff. She kind of liked me, but felt obligated to bite me because of the company I kept (as we shall see, she had good reason to dislike my entourage – especially one of them). I would whisk my hand away in the nick of time; her jaws would snap shut on empty air; I would bid her *à plus tard* and wish her better luck tomorrow. I would hate to think I was tormenting her. It was just a game –

and I was really curious to see how long it would be before she stopped trying to bite me. She never did.

In any event, I've never been afraid of dogs. And this transferred naturally to wolves. I greeted Yukon in the way I would an unfamiliar Great Dane – relaxed and friendly, but nonetheless observing the standard protocols. Yukon turned out to be nothing like Blue, or even my friend the Dogo. He was a good-natured wolf, confident and outgoing. But misunderstandings can, of course, arise even with the best animals. The most typical reason for a dog to bite – and I suspect a similar story can be told for wolves – is that they lose track of your hand. People reach around to pat the back of the dog's head or neck. Losing sight of your hand, the dog becomes nervous, suspects you might be attacking it and, accordingly, bites. It's a fear bite – the most common sort. So I let Yukon sniff my hand, and petted him at the front of his neck and chest until he became used to me. We got on like a house on fire.

Brenin's mother, Sitka – named, I assume, after the variety of spruce tree – was as tall as Yukon, but far rangier and nowhere near as massive. She looked more like a wolf, at least like all the pictures of wolves I had seen – long and lean. There are numerous sub-species of wolf. Sitka, I was told, was an Alaskan tundra wolf. Yukon, on the other hand, was a McKenzie valley wolf, from the north-west of Canada. Their different physical characteristics reflected their membership of these different sub-species.

Sitka was far too preoccupied with the six little bears she had running around her feet to pay me too much attention. And little bears is the best way I can think of describing them – round and soft and fluffy, with no sharp edges. Some of them were grey bears and some of them were brown, three males and three females. I had intended only coming to have a look at the cubs, and then going home to think carefully and soberly about whether I was ready to take on the responsibility of owning a wolf, and so on. When I saw the cubs, however, I knew I was going to take one home: today. In fact, I couldn't get my chequebook out fast enough. And when the breeder said they didn't take cheques, I couldn't drive fast enough down to the nearest ATM to get the cash.

Picking the cub was easier than I thought it was going to be. First of all, I wanted a male. There were three of those. The biggest male – indeed the biggest of the litter – was a grey, who, I could tell, was going to be the spitting image of his father. I knew enough about dogs to realize that he was going to be problematic. Utterly fearless, energetic and dominating his brother and sisters, he was destined to be the alpha male and would take some controlling. With images of Blue flashing before me, and since this was my first wolf, I decided discretion might be the better part of valour. Accordingly, I picked the second-biggest cub from the litter. He was a brown and his colouring reminded me of a little lion cub. Accordingly, I named him Brenin: the Welsh word for king. No doubt he would have been mortified if he knew he was named after a cat.

He didn't really resemble a cat in any respect. He looked more like one of those grizzly cubs you see on the Discovery Channel, following their mother around Alaska's Denali National Park. Six weeks old at this time, he was brown flecked with black, but with a cream underbelly that ran from the tip of his tail up to the bottom of his snout. And, like a bear cub, he was thick: big feet, big-boned legs and a big head. His eyes were very dark yellow, bordering on honey – and that is something that never changed. I wouldn't say he was 'friendly' – at least not in the way puppies are friendly. He was not, by any stretch of the imagination, enthusiastic, gushing or eager to please. Rather, suspicion was his pre-dominant behavioural characteristic – and, again, that was something that would never change towards anyone except me.

It's strange. I can remember all these things about Brenin and Yukon and Sitka. I can remember holding Brenin up to my face and looking in his yellow wolf eyes. I can remember the way he felt, with his soft cub fur, between my hands as I held him. I can still picture clearly Yukon standing up on his hind legs, staring down at me, big feet hanging over the stable door. I can still picture Brenin's brothers and sisters running around the pen, tumbling over each other and jumping back to their feet in glee. But of the person who sold me Brenin, I can remember virtually nothing. Something had already started; a process that would become more and more pro-nounced as the years rolled on. I was already starting to tune out human beings. When you have a wolf, they take over your life in a way that a dog seldom does. And human com-pany gradually becomes less and less significant for you. I remember the details of Brenin and his parents and siblings – how they looked, how they felt, what they did, the sounds they made. I can even remember their smell. Their details, in all their vividness, complexity, richness and glory, still stand as clear in my mind today as they did then. But of the man who owned them I remember only the outlines; the gist. I remember his story – at least I think I do – but I don't remem-ber the man.

He had moved down from Alaska, bringing a breeding pair of wolves with him. However, it is against the law – I'm not sure whether that was state or federal law – to buy, sell or own pure-blood wolves. You can buy, sell and own wolf–dog hybrids, and the highest ratio of wolf to dog allowed by law is 96 per cent. He assured me that they were, in fact, wolves, not wolf–dog hybrids. Since, a few hours earlier, I had never even known I could own a wolf–dog, I didn't really care. I paid him the $500 I had extracted from the ATM, pretty much emptying my bank account in the process, and took Brenin home with me that very afternoon. And there we began thrashing out the terms of our association.

3

After his initial destructive surge, which lasted about fifteen minutes or so, Brenin went into a deep depression, making himself a den under my desk and refusing to come out or eat. This lasted a couple of days. I assumed he was devastated at losing his brothers and sisters. I felt so sorry for him, and very guilty. I wished I could have bought a brother or sister to keep him company, but I simply didn't have the money. In a day or two, however, his mood began to lift. And, when it did, the first rule of our mutual accommodation became clear – very clear, in fact. The rule was that Brenin was never, ever, under any circumstances, to be left on his own in the house. Failure to abide by this rule involved dire consequences for the house and its contents; and the fate of the curtains and the air-conditioning pipes was merely a gentle warning of his true capabilities in this regard. These consequences included destruction of all furniture and carpets, with a soiling option also available for the latter. Wolves, I learned, get bored very, very quickly – about thirty seconds of being left to their own devices is generally long enough.

When Brenin got bored he would either chew on things or urinate on them, or chew on things and then urinate on them. Very occasionally, he would even urinate on things and then chew them, but I think that was just because, in all the excitement, he would forget exactly where he was in the order of proceedings. But the upshot was that wherever I went Brenin had to go too.

Of course, when the 'I' in question is a wolf, the rule 'wherever you go I go too' precludes most forms of gainful employment. That is just one reason, one of many, never to find yourself owning a wolf. However, I was lucky. To begin with, I was a university professor – and I really didn't have to go into work very often anyway. Even better, Brenin arrived during the university's three-month-long summer hiatus, and so I didn't have to go into work at all. This gave me ample time both to properly recognize Brenin's immense appetite for destruction and to prepare him for the obviously obligatory journeys into work with me.

Some people say you can't train wolves. They're actually quite wrong; you can pretty much train anything if you find the right method – that is the hard part. With a wolf, there are so many ways of getting it wrong, but, as far as I know, only one way of getting it right. But that's almost true of dogs as well. Perhaps the most common misconception people have is that training has something to do with ego. They think of it as a battle of wills, where their dog has to be pressed to conform. Indeed, when we talk of someone being 'brought to heel', that is the sort of thing we have in mind. The mistake this sort of person makes is to see training as too personal. Any unwillingness on the part of their dog they then see as a personal slight – an insult to their masculinity (and it's usually a man who sees training in this way). And then, of course, they turn nasty. The first rule of dog training is, or should be, that there is nothing personal involved. Training is not a battle of wills, and if you think of it in that way, it is going to go disastrously wrong. If you are trying to train a big, aggressive dog in this way, he will, in all likelihood, grow up to be not very nice at all.

The opposite mistake is to think that your dog's obedience can be obtained not through domination but by rewards. The rewards can take different forms. Some people obsessively pop treats into the mouths of their dogs for accomplishing even the easiest of tasks. The most obvious result of this is a fat dog that will refuse to obey its owner when it suspects there is no treat around to be offered, or when it is distracted by something – a cat, another dog, a jogger, etc. – that it deems more interesting than a treat. More often, however, the 'reward' takes the form of an inane chatter they insist in carrying on with their dog. 'Good boy' . . . 'Aren't you a clever boy, then?' . . . 'This way' . . . 'Heel' . . . 'What a clever dog you are' – and so on and so forth. And they often accompany this chatter with nagging little tugs on the lead to, as they see it, help reinforce their message. This is, in fact, precisely the way not to train a dog – and it hasn't a snowball's chance in hell of working with a wolf. If you're continually talking to your dog, or half-heartedly tugging on his lead, he has no need to watch you. In fact, he has no reason to give a fig about what you're doing. He can do what he likes in the sure knowledge that you will let him know what's happening – and that he can act on or disregard this information as he chooses.

People who think that their dog's obedience can be bought are people who think – and how often have I heard this – that their dog basically wants to do as his 'master' wants – he always aims to please – and simply needs to have explained to him precisely what this is. And this is, of course, non-sense. Your dog doesn't want to obey you any more than you want to obey anyone else. Why should he? The key to train-ing your dog is to make him think he has no choice in the matter. This is not because he is made to feel the loser in a battle of wills, but because of an attitude of calm but remorse-less inevitability that you must bring to your training. In a battle of wills, you are saying to the wolf: you will do what I say – I am giving you no choice. But the attitude with which to train a wolf is: you will do what the situation demands – this situation affords no other option. It is not I to whom you are responding; it is the world. Maybe it's scant consolation for the wolf. But it certainly helps put the trainer in his or her proper place – not as a dominant and arbitrary authority whose will is to be obeyed at all costs, but as an educator who allows the wolf to understand what the world requires of it. Of all the methods of training a dog, it is the Koehler method that elevates this attitude to an art form.

When I was a kid – around six or seven – I used to go to Saturday morning cinema shows with my friends. I would be given 10p by my mum and we would walk a couple of miles into town. It cost 5p to get into the cinema and 3½p for a can of MacCola, sold, improbably enough, not by McDonald's – they hadn't reached Wales at this time – but by the fishmon-ger chain MacFisheries. I remember only one film from those days and only one scene from that film. This was the scene in *The Swiss Family Robinson* where the somewhat unwel-come advances of a tiger are rebuffed by the family's two Great Danes. The scene obviously made a great impression on me – no doubt because I grew up with Great Danes. The scene was the work of an animal trainer, William Koehler.

My six-year-old self would never have believed – but would undoubtedly have been delighted – that in twenty years' time I would be using Koehler's methods to train a wolf.

This came about through one of the fortuitous coincidences that have casually littered my life. A few months earlier, I had stumbled across a book in the University of Alabama library: Vicki Hearne's *Adam's Task*. Hearne was a professional animal trainer who combined her profession with an amateur interest in philosophy. There are not too many of those around. It is safe to say that she was a better animal trainer than philosopher – the philosophy seemed to consist largely of a somewhat confused version of the sort of philosophy of language developed by the Austrian philosopher Ludwig Wittgenstein. Nevertheless, I found her book both interesting and suggestive. If her philosophy of language was confused, one thing she was unequivocal about was that, by a country mile, the best dog trainer around was William Koehler. When Brenin arrived on the scene, therefore, I had a good idea where to turn – philosophical solidarity, if nothing else, dictated it.

Between you and me, Koehler was a bit of a psychopath. And, in places, his training involves certain excesses that I personally have no interest in pursuing. For example, if your dog persists in digging holes in the garden, Koehler's instructions are to fill the hole with water and duck your dog's head in it. And then – get this – continue for five days, irrespective of whether your dog has dug any more holes. The idea is to create in your dog an aversion to holes. The method is based on sound behaviourist principles, and would almost certainly work. It's presumably the sort of method the US military adapted for torturing insurgents, and some unlucky bystanders, in Abu Ghraib. (I didn't find any reference to waterboarding your dog in Koehler's book, but I suspect he would have approved.)

Koehler's advice would actually have stood me in good stead during Brenin's den-digging phase – a 'phase' that lasted the best part of four years – during which time my garden – actually, there was more than one garden involved – was transformed into something resembling the Somme. But I never had the heart to use it: I always liked Brenin a lot more than my garden. And, anyway, the trench-warfare land-scaping actually possessed a certain charm that grew on me after a while.

However, if you strip away its excesses, you will find that the Koehler method, in general, is based on a very simple, and effective, principle: your dog/wolf must be made to watch you. The key to training Brenin – and I am eternally grateful to Koehler for being right about this – was to calmly but remorselessly make him have to watch me. Getting the animal to look at what you are doing, and so take its lead from you, is the cornerstone of any training regime – whether that animal is a wolf or a dog. But it is especially important in a wolf, and it is a more difficult thing to get a wolf to do. Dogs do it naturally; but wolves have to be persuaded to do it. The reasons for this can be found in their different histories.

4

Over the past few decades there have been a number of stud-ies conducted with the aim of gauging which are the most intelligent, dogs or wolves. These studies, in my view, all converge on a single answer: neither. The intelligence of wolves and dogs is different because it has been shaped by different environments and is, therefore, a response to different needs and requirements. Generally, the picture is this: wolves do better than dogs on problem tasks, while dogs do better than wolves on training tasks.

A problem task is one that requires the animal to engage in some form of means–end reasoning. For example, Harry Frank, a professor of psychology at the University of Michigan-Flint, reports on how one of his wolves learned to open the door from its kennels into the outside compound. To be opened, the handle of the door first had to be pushed towards the door and then it had to be rotated. Frank reports that a dog – a malamute – that also lived at the facility watched them do this several times a day for six years and never learned how to do it himself. A malamute–wolf hybrid acquired the skill after two weeks. But the wolf learned the task after watching the hybrid once. And she didn't use the same technique as the hybrid: he used his muzzle, she used her paws. This seems to show that she understood the nature of the problem, and what had to be done to solve it, and was not merely copying the behaviour of the hybrid.

Test after test has conformed that wolves outshine dogs in these sorts of means–end reasoning cases. Dogs, however, outshine wolves on tests that require instruction or training. In one test of this sort, for example, dogs and wolves were required to execute a right turn whenever a light flashed. Dogs could be trained to do this; but wolves, apparently, could not – at least not for the duration of the tests.

In the first case, the problem to be solved is a mechanical one. The desired end is getting out into the compound, and there is one and only one means available to achieving this end: the door handle has to be manipulated in an appropriate way and order. But in the training test, there is no mechanical relationship between the flashing light and a right turn. Why a right turn and not a left? Why a turn at all? The connection between the flashing light and the subsequent required behaviour is an arbitrary one.

It is easy to see why there should be this difference between wolves and dogs. Wolves live in a mechanical world. If, for example, there is a fallen tree balanced precariously on a boulder, then the wolf can see that walking underneath it is a bad idea. It can see this because, in the past, wolves that could not see this would be far more likely to be crushed by falling objects than those that could. Therefore wolves that could not understand the relationship between the tree, the rock and possible danger would be less likely to pass on their genes than those who could. The environment of the wolf, in this way, selects for mechanical intelligence.

Contrast this with the world of the dog. The dog lives in what is for him a magical world rather than a mechanical one. When I travel for work, I'll call home to talk to my wife, Emma. Nina, our German shepherd—malamute cross, gets very excited when she hears my voice and starts bouncing around and barking. And if Emma holds out the phone, Nina will lick it enthusiastically. Dogs are comfortable with magic. Who would have thought that the voice of the pack's alpha male could materialize from nowhere whenever someone holds up that funny-shaped thing on the desk? There again, who would have thought that flipping a switch on the wall would transform darkness into light? The world of the dog makes no mechanical sense. And even if it did, the means of controlling it are outside the dog's abilities. It cannot reach the light switch. It cannot dial a phone number. And it cannot insert a key into a lock.

I have to be careful here and not become carried away, or you're liable to get a lecture on embodied and embedded cognition. In my professional life, what I'm probably most known for is being one of the architects of a view of the mind that sees it as essentially embodied and embedded in the world around it. Mental activities do not just take place inside our heads – they are not just brain processes. Rather, they also involve activities we do in the world: in particular, the manipulation, transformation and exploitation of relevant environmental structures. And already the lecture is in full swing. The forerunner of this view was the Soviet psychologist Lev Vygotsky, who, with his colleague Anton Luria, demonstrated just how much processes of remembering and other mental activities had changed with the development of an external device for storing information. The outstanding natural memory of primitive cultures gradually withers away as we rely more and more on written language as a way of storing our memories. On an evolutionary timescale, the development of written language is, of course, a very recent phenomenon. Nonetheless, its effect on memory and other mental activities has been profound.

To cut a long lecture short, the dog has been embedded in a very different environment from the wolf. Therefore its psychological processes and abilities have developed in very different ways. In particular, the dog has been forced to rely on us. More than that, it has developed the ability to use us to solve its various problems, cognitive and otherwise. For dogs, we are useful information-processing devices. We humans are part of the dog's extended mind. When a dog faces a mechanical problem it finds impossible to solve, what does it do? It enlists our help. As I write this sentence, I am provided with a simple yet vivid example of this principle. Nina wants to go out into the garden. Not being able to open the door herself, she stands by the door and looks at me. If I hadn't seen her, she would have given a little bark. Clever girl. The environment of the wolf has selected for mechanical intelligence. But the environment of the dog has selected for the ability to use us. And to use us they have to be able to read us. When an intelligent dog is faced with an insoluble problem, the first thing it will do is look at its owner's face. Encultured into a world of magic, this comes naturally to the dog. But a wolf will not do this. The key to training a wolf is getting it to do so.

5

Of course, this is all after-the-fact rationalization. I didn't know any of it then. Brenin was an old wolf by the time I published my first book on this sort of stuff. And I'm still trying to refine the view. But it is interesting that a theory I should only develop many years later should allow me to understand just why the method I had chosen to train my wolf should be so effective – and I can't help thinking the process of training got me thinking, on some unconscious level, in the right sort of way to later develop the theory. If so, this might be another of those aforementioned fortuitous coincidences.

Following the Koehler method, then, Brenin's training began like this. I acquired a fifteen-foot piece of rope which I fashioned into a leash. We would go out into the large back garden and I would set up three clearly visible markers – in this case, long wooden stakes hammered into the ground. I would attach the rope to Brenin's choke-chain. Don't let anyone tell you that choke-chains are cruel: they are essential for effective training since they communicate to a dog exactly what is required of him. The message sent by ordinary collars is far less precise and training will take longer as a result. I would walk from one marker to the next – at times of my own choosing and selecting markers at random. I did this impassively, without looking at Brenin or even acknowledging his presence.

One component of a successful and intelligent training programme is to always put yourself in the shoes of your dog. It's ironic, and to me highly amusing, that some philosophers still question whether animals have minds – whether they can think, believe, reason, even feel. They should try getting their noses out of their books and train a dog some time. The training programme will always throw something unexpected at you. Your dog won't do what he's supposed to; and you won't be able to find the answer in the book – even in one as thoughtful and comprehensive as Koehler's. Then the only recourse you have is to try and think like your dog. If you do that, you can usually work out what you should do.

Put yourself in Brenin's shoes. If he charges off in one direction, he is going to have fifteen feet of rope to get up a fair head of steam, but then will be snapped to a sharp halt. The effect is exacerbated if he is charging in one direction when I'm walking in another. Soon – very soon – he works out that if he is to avoid this unpleasantness he is going to have to watch where I am going. Initially, he tries to do his watching from the limits of the leash. But this makes him vulnerable to me performing a sharp turn away from him, which I then do. So he comes closer to me. Now he tries to walk a little in front of me – but far enough back to see what

I am doing out of the corner of his eye. This, apparently, is entirely typical. I rectified this by turning sharply into him, driving my knee – impassively rather than savagely – into his ribs. So then he starts walking behind me – clever boy. I corrected this by stopping sharply and walking back into him, treading on his feet if possible. Then, understandably, he tries walking as far as he can from me. But now he is again at or near the extent of the leash – and this makes him vulnerable to my making a sharp turn away from him – a turn that I, of course, now perform. And so we are back at the beginning. This is all done in silence and completely dispassionately. That is the calm but remorseless face of Koehler's method. There is nothing personal in a wolf's mistakes and you must never ever lose your temper with them. Very soon, Brenin has exhausted all the possible ways of not cooperating with me. All that is left for him is cooperation. And so he walks to heel.

People – including people who owned wolves – told me that it was impossible to train a wolf to walk on a leash. Those are the sorts of people who keep their wolves, wolf–dogs or dogs locked up in a run in the back garden. And that, I believe, is a criminal act for which a custodial sentence would be appropriate (and, of course, it would certainly help them put themselves in their wolf's shoes). It actually took no more than two minutes to get Brenin to walk on a leash. Other people told me it was impossible to train a wolf to walk to heel. That took a further ten minutes.

Once we had mastered the basics of on-leash walking, teaching Brenin to walk off leash was surprisingly easy – because, crucially, he already understood what he was supposed to do. First, we worked with the leash still attached to him but without me holding on to it. Then, when that was successful, we progressed to walking without the leash altogether. Here, the use of a throw-chain is essential. This is a smaller version of his choke-chain – actually I used a choke-chain designed for a small dog. If Brenin broke away from heel, I first rattled the throw-chain and then hurled it at him. When hit, the pain would be sharp, but quickly dissipate. And, of course, no lasting damage would be done. How do I know this? Because, being a little circumspect about this part of the Koehler programme, I had a friend throw the chain at me a few times first. Quite quickly Brenin came to associate the rattle of the chain with the unpleasantness to follow, and there was no further need to throw the chain at him. It took four days (two thirty-minute sessions per day) to train him to walk to heel off a leash.

I taught Brenin only what I thought he needed to know. I never saw the point of teaching him tricks. If he didn't feel like rolling over, why should I require him to do so? I didn't even bother teaching him to sit – whether he sat or stood was, as far as I was concerned, an entirely personal decision. Walking to heel quickly became his default behaviour. There were only four other things he needed to know:

Off you go and sniff around – '*Go on!*'
Stay where you are – '*Stay!*'
Come to me – '*Here!*'

And most important of all:

Leave it alone – '*Out!*'

The pronunciation of each was guttural, like a growl. Later we worked on finger clicks and hand signals. By the time the summer was over Brenin was fairly – I wouldn't say thoroughly, but he was getting there – proficient in this basic verbal and non-verbal language.

I know: I'm far too smug about this. But this training was the greatest gift I ever gave Brenin – a shining example of one of the few things in my life I really did right. Some people think that training dogs – and, even more so, wolves – is cruel, as if you are going to break their spirit or make them permanently cowed. But far from breaking his spirit, when a dog or wolf knows exactly what is and what is not expected of him his confidence, and as a result his composure, grow immensely. It is a hard truth that, as Friedrich Nietzsche once put it, those who can't discipline themselves will quickly find somebody else doing it for them. And, for Brenin, it was my responsibility to be that somebody. But the relation between discipline and freedom is a deep and important one: far from being opposed to freedom, discipline is what makes the most worthwhile forms of freedom possible. Without discipline there is no real freedom; there is only licence.

On our walks over the next decade or so we would sometimes meet dog owners who always kept their dogs – often these were wolf-like dogs such as huskies and malamutes – on leads, claiming that otherwise the dogs would charge off into the distance and they would never get them back on the lead or possibly even see them again. This may well have been true. But it certainly didn't have to be that way. Later, when we lived in Ireland, we walked every day through fields of sheep with Brenin unleashed. I was, admittedly, a little nervous the first time we tried it – though possibly not as nervous as the sheep. And during the whole of our time together, I never had to shout at Brenin; and I never hit him. One thing of which I'm fairly certain is that if a wolf can be trained to completely ignore his archetypal prey, then any dog can be trained to come when called.

As you will see, Brenin would go on to lead what was, for a wolf, almost certainly an unprecedented life. He led this life because I could, and therefore did, take him everywhere I went. Admittedly, the impetus for this was Brenin's capacity to reduce my house to rubble on any given unattended morning while I did my lecturing. But the possibility of our living together in any meaningful way – in contrast to him being stuck out in the back garden and forgotten – was provided by him learning a language. This language gave his life a structure it otherwise could not have had and because of this revealed a canvas of possibilities it otherwise could not have contained. Brenin learned a language, and given that he was going to be living in a human world, a magical world rather than a mechanical one, this language set him free.

6

An unprecedented life, of course, is not necessarily a good one. I was sometimes asked: how could you do this? How could I take an animal out of its natural environment and force it to live a life that it must have found completely unnatural? It was almost always a particular kind of person who asked this question: a middle-class liberal academic with green pretensions who had no history or knowledge of dog ownership. But casting aspersions on the person who asks the question, rather than looking at the question itself, is what's known in philosophy as an *ad hominem* fallacy. The question itself is a good one and should be addressed.

First of all, I suppose I could point out that Brenin was

born in captivity not in the wild, and without the requisite training from his parents would have quickly perished had he been 'released' into the wild. But this response doesn't get me very far. By paying money for Brenin, I was perpetuating a system that saw wolves bred in captivity, thus depriving them of the opportunity to act as nature had intended. So the question then is: how could I justify doing this?

What underpins the question is, I think, this belief: a wolf can only be truly happy or fulfilled doing what nature intended it to do – engaging in its natural behaviours like hunting and interacting with other pack members. This claim may seem obviously true, but is, in fact, difficult to pin down. First of all, there is the rather tricky idea of what nature intended. What does nature intend for a wolf? Or, for that matter, what does it intend for a human? Indeed, in what sense can nature intend anything at all? In evolutionary theory, we sometimes talk, metaphorically, of what nature intends, but such talk basically amounts to this: nature 'intends' creatures to propagate their genes. The only concrete sense that can be given to the idea of nature's intentions is grounded in the concept of genetic success. Hunting and the life of the pack are strategies employed by animals like wolves in order to satisfy this basic biological imperative. Even wolves, however, can adopt different strategies. At one point in their history, for reasons that are still unclear, wolves attached themselves to human packs and became dogs. To the extent that nature has intentions at all, this was part of her intentions no more and no less than wolves remaining wolves.

This is a useful trick I learned from philosophy: when someone makes a claim, try and work out what are the presuppositions of this claim. So, if someone says that wolves can be happy only engaging in natural behaviours such as hunting and interacting with their pack, what are the presuppositions of this claim? When we look at the presuppositions, what I think we find are, at least for the most part, expressions of human arrogance.

Jean-Paul Sartre once tried to define the idea of a human being by saying that for humans, and humans alone, their existence precedes their essence. This was the foundational principle of the philosophical movement that became known as existentialism. The being of humans, Sartre claimed, is being-for-itself; and this contrasts with the being of everything else, which is merely being-in-itself. As Sartre unhelpfully put it, humans are the beings who have their being to be. What he meant was that humans have to choose how to live their lives and cannot rely on any pre-given rules or principles – religious, moral, scientific or otherwise – telling them how to do it. To adopt a particular principle, a moral or religious maxim for example, is an expression of choice. So, no matter what you do and no matter how you live, this is always ultimately an expression of your free will. Humans are, as Sartre put it, condemned to be free.

The other side of the coin is that, for Sartre, everything else is not free. Other things, even other living things, can do only what they have been designed to do. If countless millennia of evolution have shaped wolves into hunting, pack-living animals, then this provides the only viable form of life for them. A wolf does not have its being to be. A wolf can only be what it is. The presupposition that underlies our question – how could you do this to Brenin? – is, then, this: a wolf's essence precedes its existence.

Of course, it's not clear that Sartre was right about human freedom. But what I'm interested in is this more general idea of existential flexibility. Why should it be that humans, and only humans, are capable of living their lives in myriad different ways, while every other creature is condemned to be a slave of its biological heritage – a mere servant of its natural history? Upon what can this idea be based other than a residual form of human arrogance? A couple of years ago I was sitting in the beer garden of a hotel not far from Gatwick Airport the evening before an early-morning flight to Athens. A fox came up to me and sat down like a dog no more than a few feet away, patiently waiting to see if I would throw it a few scraps of food – which, of course, I did. The waitress told me he (or she) was a regular fixture at the hotel – and apparently some of the other hotels too. Try telling this fox that it should be engaged in its natural behaviour of hunting mice. Try telling this fox that its essence precedes its existence and that, unlike me, it doesn't have its being to be.

We demean the fox when we think of its natural behaviour as restricted to hunting mice. We demean its intelligence and its resourcefulness when we adopt such a restrictive conception of, as Sartre would put it, its being. What is natural for the fox is continually shifting with the vicissitudes of history and fortune. And, therefore, so too is the being of the fox – what the fox is.

Of course, you cannot simply dismiss the constraints of natural history. The fox would be neither happy nor fulfilled sitting day after day in a cage. Neither would a wolf. And neither would I. We all have certain basic needs bequeathed us by our history. But it would be a non sequitur to suppose that the wolf and the fox are merely biological marionettes whose strings are pulled by their history. Their essence may constrain their existence, but it does not fix or determine it. This is as true of the fox and the wolf as it is of us. In life, we each play the hand we have been dealt. Sometimes the hand is so bad we can do nothing at all with it. But sometimes it is not – and then we can play it well or badly. The hand dealt the fox was rapid urban encroachment on to what we like to think of as its natural habitat – although it has, I think, been a very, very long time since that nomenclature made any real sense. My friend the fox, I suspect, was playing his hand rather well, judging by the way he progressed from table to table – but only the tables where there was food – sitting patiently until the requisite offerings had been made.

Brenin, too, was dealt a certain hand, and I think he played it pretty well. It wasn't really that bad a hand anyway. He could have ended up, like so many wolves and wolf hybrids whose owners cannot handle them, in a cage in the backyard. Instead, he had a varied and, I would like to think, stimulating life. I made sure he had at least one long walk every day – and his training permitted this to be off leash. When circumstances permitted, I made sure he had the opportunity to engage in natural behaviours like hunting and interacting with other canines. I did my best to make sure that he was never bored – the chore of sitting through my lectures notwithstanding. To suppose that Brenin could not be happy simply because he was not doing what natural wolves do is little more than a banal form of human arrogance, and belittles his intelligence and flexibility.

Brenin was, of course, following in the footsteps of his ancestors of some 15,000 years ago – echoing the call of the civilized that drew them into a symbiotic, and perhaps unbreakable, relationship with the most powerful and vicious of the great apes. In terms of genetic success, you have only to count the number of wolves in the world today versus the number of dogs – roughly 400,000 versus 400 million – to understand that this was a breathtakingly successful strategy.

And to suppose that this is an unnatural thing for a wolf to do betrays a pretty facile understanding of what is natural. When you add to this the rather abbreviated lifespan of wolves in the wild – seven years is going some – and the typically unpleasant manner of their deaths, then the call of the civilized was perhaps not an unmitigated disaster.

I think the Koehler method that I used to train Brenin was ultimately so successful because it resonates with a certain understanding of the existential nature of dogs and their wild brothers. This was hidden by my caricatural dismissal of some of its excesses. Animating the Koehler method is a kind of faith. It is the faith that the essence of a dog, or a wolf, does not precede its existence. It is the faith that a dog, or a wolf, has its being to be no more and no less than a human being. Because of this, it is necessary to accord any dog or wolf a certain kind of respect and, on the basis of that, a certain kind of right – a moral right. This, as Koehler puts it, is 'the right to the consequences of its actions'. A wolf is not a puppet made flesh, blindly following the dictates of its biological heritage – at least no more than human beings are. A wolf is adaptable – not infinitely adaptable, but then what is? A wolf, no less than a human, can play the hand it has been dealt. And, what is more, you can help it to do this. As it becomes better at playing this hand, it becomes more confident. It enjoys what it learns and wants to learn more. It becomes stronger and consequently happier.

Was Brenin a slave? Was he a slave because I set the parameters of his education and so determined the contours of his future action? Does the fact that I spent seven years at a 'bog standard' comprehensive school, followed by three years at Manchester and two years at Oxford universities – where the parameters of my education were very definitely set by other people – make me a slave? If Brenin was a slave, then so too am I. But if so, what does the word 'slave' mean? If we are all slaves, then who is the master? And if there is no master, then who is the slave?

Perhaps this argument isn't as good as I think it is. Perhaps my judgement is clouded by everything Brenin did for me. Some people get dogs and, after the novelty has worn off, basically stick them out in the back garden and forget about them. Then the dog becomes nothing more than a chore. They have to be fed and watered, and that's the only interaction these people will have with their dogs – something boring, something they don't feel like doing but figure they should do. Some people even think that as long as they regularly feed and water their dog they're being good owners. If that is the way you feel about it, why bother getting a dog? You get nothing out of it, only the daily irritation of having to do something you really don't feel like doing. But when a dog lives in your house with you, when he inserts himself into your life so completely that he becomes part of that life, that is where all the joy is found. Having a dog is like any relationship: you only get out of it what you are willing to put in – and willing to allow in. The same is true of a wolf. But because a wolf is not a dog – because a wolf has foibles that a dog does not – you have to work so much harder at bringing him in.

7

Brenin and I were inseparable for eleven years. Homes would change, jobs would change, countries and even continents would change, and my other relationships would come and go – mostly go. But Brenin was always there – at home, at work and at play. He was the first thing I would see in the morning when I woke – largely because he would be the one to wake me, around daybreak with a big wet lick to the face – a looming presence of meaty breath and sandpaper tongue framed by dawn's murky light. And that was on a good day – on bad days he would have caught and killed a bird in the garden and would wake me up by dropping it on my face. (The first rule of living with a wolf: always expect the unexpected.) He would lie under my desk while I wrote in the mornings. He would walk or run with me almost every day of his life. He would come into class with me while I did my lecturing in the afternoons. And he would sit with me in the evenings while I worked my way through innumerable bottles of Jack Daniel's.

It was not just that I loved having him around – although I did. Much of what I learned, about how to live and how to conduct myself, I learned during those eleven years. Much of what I know about life and its meaning I learned from him. What it is to be human: I learned this from a wolf. And so thoroughly did he insert himself into every facet of my life, so seamlessly did our lives become intertwined, that I came to understand, even define, myself in terms of my relationship to Brenin.

Some people say that owning pets is wrong because it makes them your property. Technically, I suppose this is true. There is some minimal legal sense in which I could be said to have been the owner of Brenin – although since, for much of his life, I didn't have any sort of documents recording ownership, it is not clear how I could have demonstrated this in a court of law. But I have never been convinced by this objection, because it is, in effect, a non sequitur. It assumes that if you are the owner of something in a legal sense, then this is the only relationship you can ever have with it; or, at the very least, ownership is the dominant relationship you have with it. But there is, in fact, little reason for believing this.

Fundamentally, Brenin was not my property; and he was certainly not my pet. He was my brother. Sometimes, and in some respects, he was my younger brother. At those times, and in those respects, I was his guardian; protecting him from a world that he did not understand and that did not trust him. At those times, I had to make decisions about what we were going to do, and enforce the decisions whether or not Brenin consented to them. At this point some of my friends in the animal rights movement will start bleating about unequal power relations and how, since Brenin could not give his consent to my decisions, he was, in effect, my prisoner. But, again, this charge doesn't seem very plausible. Imagine my brother was human rather than lupine. If he was too young to understand the world, and the consequences of his actions in that world, then I could not simply abandon him to those consequences. As we saw, Koehler championed the dog's right to the consequences of its actions. I agree; but this right is, of course, not an absolute right. It is what philosophers call a prima facie right: a right that can be overridden in appropriate circumstances. If your dog was about to run out in front of a car, perhaps because it had ignored your instructions, then you would not simply allow it to suffer the consequences of its actions. On the contrary, you would do your best to make sure that it avoided those consequences. And the same would be true if my younger brother were about to run out in front of a car. Within the limitations imposed by common sense and general human decency, when the consequences are not too severe or debilitating, I would allow my younger brother to suffer or enjoy the consequences of his actions, because that is the only way in which he will learn. But in other circumstances, I would have to protect him the best I could, even if he did not consent to this protection. To say that this would make him my prisoner seems to be the result of an overly excitable determination to ignore the distinction between guardianship and imprisonment.

It is the concept of guardianship rather than ownership that seems to provide the most plausible way of understanding the primary relationship between people – at least decent people – and their companion animals. But, with Brenin, this doesn't quite seem to fit either. This is what distinguished him – decisively – from any dog I have ever known. It was only at some times, and in some circumstances, that Brenin was my younger brother. At other times, and in other circumstances, he was my older brother: a brother that I admired and wanted, above all, to emulate. As we shall see, this was no easy task, and I never achieved more than a fraction of it. But it was the attempt, and the resulting struggle, that forged me. The person I became, I am utterly convinced, is better than the one I would otherwise have been. And nothing more can be asked of an older brother.

There are different ways of remembering. When we think of memory, we overlook what is most important in favour of what is most obvious. A bird does not fly by flapping its wings; this is merely what provides it with forward propulsion. The real principles of flight are to be found in the shape of the bird's wings, and the resulting differences in the pressure of the air flowing over the upper and lower surfaces of those wings. But in our early attempts to fly, we overlooked what is most important in favour of what is most obvious: we built flapping machines. Our understanding of memory is similar. We think of memory as conscious experiences whereby we recall past events or episodes. Psychologists call this episodic memory.

Episodic memory, I think, is just the flapping of wings, and it is always the first to betray us. Our episodic memory is not particularly reliable at the best of times – decades of psychological research converge on this conclusion – and is the first to fade as our brains begin their long but inexorable descent into indolence, like the flapping of a bird's wings that gradually fades in the distance.

But there is another, deeper and more important way of remembering: a form of memory that no one ever thought to dignify with a name. This is the memory of a past that has written itself on you, in your character and in the life on which you bring that character to bear. You are not, at least not typically, aware of these memories; often they are not even the sorts of things of which you can be conscious. But they, more than anything else, make you what you are. These memories are exhibited in the decisions you make, the actions you take and the life that you thereby live.

It is in our lives and not, fundamentally, in our conscious experiences that we find the memories of those who are gone. Our consciousness is fickle and not worthy of the task of remembering. The most important way of remembering someone is by being the person they made us – at least in part – and living the life they have helped shape. Sometimes they are not worth remembering. In that case, our most important existential task is to expunge them from the narrative of our lives. But when they are worth remembering, then being someone they have helped fashion and living a life they have helped forge are not only how we remember them; they are how we honour them.

I will always remember my wolf brother.

3

Distinctly Uncivilized

1

In late August Brenin and I headed into the University of Alabama for our first class together. The summer had seen him grow up fast and strong and big. From a chubby little bear, he had become long, lean and angular. Although he was not quite six months old yet, he was already thirty inches at the shoulder and weighed around eighty pounds. I used to weigh him, much to his chagrin, by picking him up and standing with him on the bathroom scales. And the days were drawing to a close when I could do that – not so much because I couldn't lift him, but because we were collectively getting too heavy for the scales. His colour had remained the same: he was brown, flecked with black, with a cream under-belly. He had inherited the big snowshoe feet of his parents and always gave the impression that he was about to trip over them. He never did. There was a black line that ran down the dorsal edge of his snout, from his head to his nose, and this was framed by his eyes, still the colour of almond; eyes that had now taken on the hooded, slanting shape of a wolf's. In those early days he could barely contain the power he must have felt coursing through his body. I had nicknamed him 'Buffalo Boy', because of his habit of charging around the house at full tilt, knocking over any household items that weren't screwed to the ground (and some that were). During the summer months, our departures from the house had slowly developed into something bordering on ritual. I would announce our departure by saying, 'Let's go.' This would be the cue for him to initiate his party piece: a cartwheel that he would perform on the living-room wall. His method involved running at and jumping on to the settee, then continuing his run up the wall. When he had got as high as he could, he would swing his back legs up and around, then run back down the wall. It was the same story every time we went out. Often Brenin would do his trick before I had said anything at all, as if to let me know that we had people to see and places to go. So I think we can safely say that it was with some trepidation that I drove into the university for that first class.

In fact, there were no major disasters that morning. I had tired him out with a long walk before we went in, and after he had become used to there being other people in the room, he lay down under the table at the front of the room and went to sleep. He did wake up and start attacking my sandals around about the time I was running through Descartes's arguments for doubting the existence of the external world. But I think everyone agreed this was a welcome distraction.

Things didn't always go so smoothly. There would be the occasional mishap. After a few weeks, he started to enjoy a

post-nap howling session halfway through the class, possibly
to register his general dissatisfaction with the way the class
was proceeding. A quick glance in the direction of the students confirmed that they knew exactly what he was talking
about. At other times, he would decide to stretch his legs,
wandering up and down the aisles, having a little sniff
around. One day, when he was feeling particularly bold or
hungry, or both, I saw his head disappear into the backpack
of a female philosophy major – someone who was, I think it
is fair to say, a little nervous around dogs at the best of
times – to emerge, a few seconds later, with her lunch.
Predicting a rash of potential compensation claims from
hungry students, I was subsequently forced to insert a clause
in the syllabus that I handed out to students at the beginning
of the course: a trio of sentences that, I'm pretty sure, had
never before appeared on any philosophy syllabus ever written. Immediately following the sections on reading materials
and assessment procedures, there would be a paragraph that
read as follows:

> **Caution:** Please do not pay any attention to the wolf.
> He will not hurt you. However, if you do have any
> food in your bags, please make sure that those bags are
> securely fastened shut.

When I think back, it was a miracle there were no com-
plaints – or, for that matter, litigation.

In the afternoons, I switched from masquerading as a lecturer to masquerading as a student. I was twenty-four years
old when I first moved to Alabama, younger than many of my
students. I had raced through my PhD at Oxford in a little
over eighteen months, which was unusually – perhaps

uniquely – quick. But the system in the US is very different. There it's a five-year slog – minimum – before you get your doctorate. And since it also takes longer – four years plus, as opposed to three – to get a bachelor's degree, this means that most Americans are not entering the academic workforce until they're pushing thirty. And this, from my perspective, was positively ancient. Since half of them were older than I was anyway, if I was looking for friends, students formed my natural constituency rather than my fellow academics. And this was no bad thing: students have a lot more fun.

So when I got to Alabama I relied on a tried and trusted strategy for acquiring a social life: team sports. I had played rugby to a fairly high level in the UK. Like most universities in the US, the University of Alabama had a rugby team – a very good one by local standards – and due to a distinct lack of rigour on the part of the USA Rugby Football Union in their procedures for checking eligibility (i.e. there weren't any), I was able to pass myself off as a student and play for the team. When Brenin came on the scene, a couple of years later, I would, of course, take him along to training with me. So most weekday afternoons we would find ourselves at Bliss Field, on the edge of the university's huge sports complex.

At weekends there would be a game against some university or other, either at home or on the road. Brenin would accompany us on all the road trips. Of course, hotels in that part of the world are, almost without exception, hostile to dogs – let alone wolves. But it was easy to sneak Brenin into motels. At a motel you park in front of your room anyway. So as long as the motel's office didn't look out on to the parking lot, lupine smuggling activities would generally go undetected. As a result, you name any major university campus in Alabama, Georgia, Florida, Louisiana, South Carolina or

Tennessee and the chances are Brenin went to a rugby match, and post-match party, there. He ate calamari on Bourbon Street in New Orleans on a balmy night in early September. He went to Daytona Beach on spring break. There's a sorority house in Baton Rouge that he knew like the back of his hand. There's a downmarket strip club on the western outskirts of Atlanta that he visited on many occasions. He even went to Vegas, courtesy of the annual Midnight Sevens rugby tournament – so called because all the games take place at night.

The rugby players soon realized something that to them was very important: Brenin was a chick magnet. In fact, they used a slightly different expression; more colourful, but not really repeatable here. Whatever we want to call it, the general insight was that if you were at a college rugby party, standing next to a large wolf, then it would be no time at all before some attractive member of the opposite sex ('rugger huggers', as they were known) approached you and said, 'I just love your dog [*sic*].' And this gave you an opening without you having to do all the usual preparatory spadework. Consequently, Brenin's presence by their side became the reward for whichever player had most distinguished himself on the field that day – the MVP (Most Valued Player), as they call them over there. I was disqualified from this competition on the grounds that I could use Brenin for such purposes any time – or so it was alleged.

During term time, we would go on road trips like this almost every other weekend – heading off on Friday afternoons, driving anywhere up to 1,000 miles round trip, playing rugby, getting very drunk and crashing in some cheap motel, before returning on Sunday afternoons, often still drunk, always exhausted, but very happy. On the other weekends there were home games, where we would do the same thing except without all the driving. And this was pretty much the life we lived – my Buffalo Boy and I – for the first four years of our association.

2

Wolves play – but not in the way dogs do. Dogs to wolves are like puppies to dogs. And the play of dogs is the result of the infantilism that has been bred into them over the course of 15,000 years. You throw a stick for your dog and the chances are he or she will tear off after it in a haze of frenzied excitement. Nina, my very intelligent German shepherd–malamute, is a sucker for sticks and she'll run after them until she drops if you let her. I did, at various times, try to convince Brenin of the delights of stick-chasing, ball-chasing and Frisbee-chasing. He would look at me as if I was mad, and his expression was easy to read: fetch? Seriously? If you want the stick so much, why don't you go and get it? Indeed, if you want it so much, why did you throw it away in the first place?

When wolves play, it is often to the consternation of passers-by, who are unable to distinguish what they are doing from fighting. I didn't realize this until years later, when I saw Brenin playing with his daughter Tess and with Nina, who had been raised by Brenin to be – stick-chasing proclivities aside – as much wolf as dog. What, by then, seemed so natural to me would arouse howls of alarm in human bystanders. For Brenin, playing amounted to seizing the other animal by the neck and pinning it to the ground. There he would proceed to shake it violently back and forth, like a rag doll. And all of this would be carried on against a background cacophony of growling and snarling. Then he would allow the other dog to wriggle free and do much the same thing to him. This is playing. I don't know why wolves play so rough, but they do. It is the growling and snarling that give the game away. They are one of the mechanisms that wolves have of reassuring their playmate that they are still playing – for their actions are so close to fighting that they might easily be misconstrued. As I discovered, when wolves really fight, they do so in utter and eerie silence.

Of course, these are all things known to a wolf but not necessarily to a dog. So Brenin's youthful attempts to initiate play with other dogs generally ended in disaster – with the other dog either attacking him or shrieking in terror. Poor Brenin must have found both responses puzzling. There was, however, one dog that totally 'got' Brenin. This was a big, uncompromising pit bull by the name of Rugger – and Rugger loved to play rough.

For a pit bull, Rugger was huge – weighing in at ninety-five pounds – and he was owned by someone who, for a human, was equally huge – Matt, one of the team's second-row forwards. Pit bulls have a bad reputation, but they are not intrinsically bad dogs. Typically, it's people who make them bad. We humans are quite comfortable with the idea that we're all different – our individuality is part of our unique charm, we like to tell ourselves. But in fact, I suspect, individuality has little to do with human uniqueness. Dogs are all different. Some are lovely; others are just plain mean. Of these, the vast majority are made mean by unfortunate conditions of nurture. This, I'm pretty sure, is what had happened to our psychotic Great Dane Blue in the first three years of his life. But some, I also think, are just born mean. Like some humans, they are mean by nature. I should stress that I'm talking about individual dogs here, not breeds. In my experience, there is a slight association between the breed of a dog and its temperament, but nothing more than that.

There was nothing very much wrong with Rugger since there was nothing very much wrong with Matt. It would not be true to say that Rugger always got Brenin. Rugger was older by a few years, and when Brenin was a cub, Rugger despised him. And, as we shall see, when Brenin got to be more than eighteen months old, this engendered a whole new raft of problems between them. But there was a window of a year or so when they were the best of friends. Most weekday afternoons, our practice would be distracted by the dazzlingly acrobatic displays of mock pugilism they would put on at the side of the field.

However, when Brenin reached eighteen months, his attitude towards other dogs began to change. If the dog was female and hadn't been spayed, then he would inevitably try to jump on her, no matter what the disparity in size between them (a cluster of traumatized West Highlands and Yorkshires and equally traumatized owners quickly learned to avoid Bliss Field on weekday afternoons). But the real problems were with male dogs. Here, his attitude was one of either contemptuous indifference or outright hostility, depending on whether he deemed the dog sufficiently large to constitute a threat. Most of the time, this was not a problem because Brenin was well trained, very obedient, and would not approach other dogs without my say-so. Occasionally, however, they would approach him, usually with a glint in their eyes, and then things would kick off.

Rugger was definitely big enough to constitute a threat. In fact, it was difficult to imagine a more impressively intimidating dog than Rugger. By the time Brenin reached maturity, they hated each other once again, and our rugby practices would see them not playing but strutting past each other, legs stiff and hackles up. Matt and I diligently kept them apart, but eventually there was the inevitable lapse. During the preparations for a game one Saturday afternoon, Rugger managed to slip the chain that attached him to Matt's pick-up. I was doing some pre-match stretching in the middle of the field and so witnessed the encounter from around thirty yards away. Rugger charged into Brenin — low, squat, all muscle and aggression. Brenin waited until the last moment and then leaped aside. He was now positioned behind Rugger and proceeded to jump on to his back and savage his neck and head. Within seconds one of Rugger's ears had largely been ripped off and blood was pouring from his face, neck and ribs. As this utterly horrifying scene unfolded, I had been sprinting in from the middle of the field. And in my terror and dismay, I instinctively jumped in and tried to pull Brenin off. This was a mistake; a potentially fatal one. Rugger used the temporary respite to lock on to Brenin's throat and would not let go.

From this I learned my first valuable lesson of dog-fighting intervention. Never pull your wolf off a pit bull. The second lesson was that if a pit bull has locked on to your wolf's throat, probably because you were stupid enough to pull your wolf off, then there is only one way of making him release. Forget about trying to prise his jaws open. That's not going to work. And forget about kicking him savagely and repeatedly in the ribs — that's not going to work either. Pour water on his face. The only way of dealing with an instinctive action — which is what the pit's locking action is — is by inducing an instinctive reaction, and water usually works. Luckily, Matt had learned this lesson before I did.

The third lesson is one I learned from subsequent quarrels:

if you do have to pull your wolf out of a fight with another dog, then grab him by the tail or the hips and, emphatically, not by the neck. If the other dog is not completely traumatized – and the sort of dog that would attack Brenin is not the sort easily traumatized – then it is going to continue its attack while your hands are placed in the vicinity of your animal's throat – which is a very bad idea. My hands and forearms still bear the patchwork of scars I acquired during the long and painful process of honing my intervention technique.

I wouldn't want to overstate Brenin's proclivity for pugilism. I could probably count the number of significant episodes on the fingers of one hand – and I'm thankful that I still have the fingers necessary to make this claim true. Brenin never inflicted serious damage on another dog – by serious, I mean anything that couldn't be cured with a few stitches here and there. Even Rugger patched up quite nicely. But this, I am pretty sure, was because I was always there to pull Brenin off. Also, it was rare for Brenin to initiate hostilities – although this may be because, given his training, he hardly ever had the opportunity. And even if another dog did approach him while my attention was distracted, a fight was easily avoided. The dog simply had to make some conventional sign of submission or abasement. The upshot was that all of Brenin's fights were with big, aggressive dogs – pits and Rottweilers were the most common – that had escaped from their owners and had no intention whatsoever of submitting to him.

It was not Brenin's enthusiasm for fighting that was the problem. It was his aptitude. If a fight occurred, I would have to wade into the middle of them and try to bring hostilities to a halt. And, not wanting any repetition of the Rugger incident, I had to try to simultaneously grab both animals. This

was, to say the least, not easy. But I had to do it, because as
long as the other dog went on fighting, Brenin would go on
fighting. And if Brenin went on fighting, the other dog would
soon be dead. His speed was blinding, his savagery breathtaking. It was difficult to reconcile this Brenin with the
animal that would wake me up in the mornings by slapping
a big wet kiss on my face; or with the animal that would, several times a day, try to climb on my lap to demand cuddles.
But I could never afford to forget that Brenin was both of
these animals.

3

Some people say that wolves, even wolf–dog hybrids, have no
place in a civilized society. After many years of reflection on
this claim, I have come to the conclusion that it's true. But it's
not true for the reasons those people think. Brenin was a dangerous animal; there is no disguising the fact. He was utterly
indifferent to other human beings – something that secretly
and selfishly delighted me. If another person tried to talk to
Brenin, or stroke him in the way you might someone else's
dog, then he would look at them inscrutably for a few seconds, then just walk away. But, in the right circumstances, he
might quickly and efficiently kill your dog. However, it is not
because he was so dangerous that there was no place for him
in a civilized society. The real reason is that he was nowhere
near dangerous, and nowhere near unpleasant, enough.
Civilization, I think, is only possible for deeply unpleasant
animals. It is only an ape that can be truly civilized.

One evening, when Brenin was around a year old, I found
myself sitting in front of the TV eating the staple diet of all

self-respecting US bachelors – a microwaveable plate of monosodium glutamate known as a Hungry Man meal. Brenin lay next to me, watching like a hawk, just in case something should tumble off the plate. The phone rang and I went to answer it, leaving the plate on the coffee table. You know when Wile E. Coyote is chasing Road Runner and he runs off the cliff? Think of the moment just after he has run off the edge, the moment when he realizes that something horrible has happened but he's not quite sure what – the moment just before he begins his mad but futile scramble back. He stands there in mid-air, frozen in place, with a look on his face that gradually transforms from enthusiasm to confusion to impending doom. It was that sort of scene that awaited me on my return to the room. Brenin, having quickly devoured my Hungry Man meal, was making his way rapidly over to his bed on the other side of the room. My return, un-welcome but not entirely unexpected, caused him to freeze in mid-stride; one leg in front of the other, his face turned towards me and gradually coalesced into a look of Wile E. apprehension. Sometimes, just before he began his plunge into the chasm, Wile E. would hold up a sign that read 'Yikes!' I'm pretty sure that if Brenin had had this sign available, he would have done the same thing.

Wittgenstein once said that if a lion could talk, we would not be able to understand him. Wittgenstein was undoubt-edly a genius. But, let's face it, he didn't really know much about lions. A wolf talks with his body; and it was clear what Brenin's body was saying: busted! You would think he might have profited from a more nonchalant, even insouciant, approach to the business of pilfering. I don't know how your plate got like that. I didn't do it. It was like that when I got here. Or even: you finished it before you left, you senile old bastard. But that is not what wolves do. They can talk. And what's more, we can understand them. What they cannot do is lie. And that is why they have no place in a civilized society. A wolf cannot lie to us; neither can a dog. That is why we think we are better than them.

4

It is a well-known fact that, relative to their body size, apes have bigger brains than wolves – almost 20 per cent bigger, in fact. So the inevitable conclusion we draw is that apes are more intelligent than wolves: simian intelligence is superior to lupine intelligence. This conclusion is not so much false as simplistic. The idea of superiority is an elliptical one. If X is superior to Y, it is always in some or other respect. So, if simian intelligence is indeed superior to lupine intelligence, we should ask ourselves: in what respect? And to answer this, we have to understand how apes acquired their bigger brains, and the price they paid for them.

At one time people used to think that intelligence was simply a matter of being able to deal with the natural world. A chimpanzee, for instance, might work out that by putting a stick into a nest of ants it can pull out the ants and eat them without getting bitten. This is an example of what I earlier called mechanical intelligence. The world presents the chimp with a problem – acquire food without being bitten – and it solves this in a mechanically intelligent way. Mechanical intelligence consists in understanding the relationship between things – in this case between a stick and the likely behaviour of ants – and using this understanding to further your purposes. As we have seen, wolves are mechanically intelligent creatures – maybe not as much as apes, but more so than dogs.

However, the brains of social creatures are, in general, larger than the brains of solitary creatures. Why would this be? The world makes the same mechanical demands on social and non-social creatures alike. The same sorts of mechanical problems arise whether you are a tiger, a wolf or an ape. The conclusion we should draw, it seems, is that mechanical intelligence is not what drives the increase in brain size. This observation provides the basis of what Andrew Whiten and Richard Byrne – two primatologists at the University of St Andrews – have called the 'Machiavellian intelligence hypothesis'. The increase in brain size, and the resulting increase in intelligence, are driven not by the demands of the mechanical world but by those of the social world.

We must be careful not to put the cart before the horse. You might think, for example, that it was their bigger brains, and resulting greater intelligence, that made some creatures realize that their lives would be better off in groups – that the group afforded them mutual support and protection. That is, they became social animals because they were more intelligent. According to the Machiavellian intelligence hypothesis, the truth is the other way around: they became more intelligent because they were social animals. The increase in brain size is not the cause of animals living together in groups; it is the effect of animals living together in groups. Social animals need to be able to do things that solitary animals do not. Mechanical intelligence might consist in understanding the relationships between things, but social animals need more than this; they need to understand the relationships between other creatures like them. This is social intelligence.

For example, an ape, monkey or wolf needs to be able to keep track of other members of its group. It needs to know who is who, and to be able to remember who is superior and who is subordinate to it. Otherwise, it doesn't behave properly and suffers as a consequence. Many insects – ants, bees, etc. – have to accomplish this trick too. But insects do it by way of the depositing and receipt of chemical messages: this was the strategy which their evolution bequeathed them. But in the social mammals another strategy was employed: an increase in intelligence of a certain sort. According to the Machiavellian intelligence hypothesis, it is the social nature of animals – and the need to keep track of social relations – that drives their increase in brain size and power, and not the other way around.

This much apes and wolves have in common. However, at some point long, long ago, apes travelled an evolutionary path that wolves did not. And the reasons for this are, to most experts, genuinely unclear. Living in groups brings with it both new possibilities and concomitant exigencies – possibilities that were never available to solitary creatures and exigencies that were never required of them. The first possibility is that of manipulating and exploiting your colleagues – and so acquiring all the benefits of group living while incurring fewer of the costs. Such manipulation and exploitation are based on a capacity for deception: the primary, and most effective, way of manipulating your colleagues is by deceiving them. The first exigency of group living, at least if you live in such a group, is a consequence of this. Since it is not good to find yourself incurring more costs and accruing fewer benefits than your fellow apes, group living is also going to require that you become smart enough to be able to tell when you are being deceived. The consequence is an escalation in intelligence driven by the imperative to deceive while not being deceived. In the evolutionary history of apes, the escalating ability to bullshit goes hand in hand with the increasing capacity to detect bullshit – with the latter, of necessity, just about outperforming the former.

There is another possibility afforded by living in groups – that of forming alliances with your peers. In ape societies, alliances are ways of using some members of your group to gang up on other members of your group. To do this, you must have the ability to scheme. But this possibility brings with it another requirement. It is not good – not conducive to your well-being and long-term prospects – to be the object of the scheming of others, the victim of one alliance after another. If others are constantly scheming against you and you want to remain part of the group, then you must constantly scheme against them. Living in certain sorts of groups brings with it the requirement to be at least as much a schemer as schemed against. In these groups the ability to scheme entails the requirement to scheme.

Scheming and deception lie at the core of the form of social intelligence possessed by apes and monkeys. For some reason, wolves never went down this path. In the pack, there is little scheming, and little deception. Some evidence seems to suggest that dogs might have the capacity for some primitive and singularly unimpressive forms of alliance building. But the evidence is inconclusive. And even if it is true, one thing is clear: with regard to these sorts of capacities, scheming and deception, dogs and wolves are like children compared to the great apes. No one really understands why apes should adopt this strategy while wolves did not. But even if we don't know why it happened, one thing is overwhelmingly clear: it did happen.

This form of intelligence, of course, reaches its apotheosis in the king of the apes: *Homo sapiens*. When we talk about the superior intelligence of apes, the superiority of simian intelligence over lupine intelligence, we should bear in mind the terms of this comparison: apes are more intelligent than wolves because, ultimately, they are better schemers and deceivers than wolves. It is from this that the difference between simian and lupine intelligence derives.

But we are apes, and we can do things of which wolves could never dream. We can create art, literature, culture, science – we can discover the truth of things. There are no wolf-Einsteins, no wolf-Mozarts and no wolf-Shakespeares. And, more modestly of course, Brenin couldn't write this book; only an ape could do that. Of course this is true. But we have to remember where all of this came from. Our scientific and artistic intelligence is a by-product of our social intelligence. And our social intelligence consists in our ability to scheme and deceive more than we are the victim of schemes and deception. This is not to say that scientific and creative intelligence simply reduce to schemes and deception. These were, presumably, the last thing on Beethoven's mind when he wrote the *Eroica*. Nor were they there in unconscious form, guiding his behaviour in a subterranean manner. I am not proposing any laughably reductionist account of Beethoven's compositional abilities. Rather, my point is that Beethoven could write the *Eroica* only because he was the product of an extended natural history that turned on the ability to lie better than one is lied to, and to plot better than one is plotted against.

We do other creatures an injustice and ourselves a disservice when we forget from where our intelligence came. It did not come for free. In our distant evolutionary past we went down a certain road, a road that wolves, for whatever reason, did not travel. We can be neither blamed nor congratulated for the road we took. There was no choice involved. In evolution, there never is. But while there is no choice involved, there are consequences. Our complexity, our sophistication, our art, our culture, our science, our truths – our, as we like to see it, greatness: all of this we purchased, and the coin was schemes and deception. Machination and mendacity lie at the core of our superior intelligence, like worms coiled at the core of an apple.

5

You may think this is a wilfully one-eyed portrayal of human distinctiveness. It may be true that we have a natural proclivity for conspiracy and duplicity. But surely we have more prepossessing features? What about love, empathy and altruism? Of course I don't contest that humans are capable of these things as well. So too, for that matter, are the great apes. But I have been trying to identify not simply what is true of human beings but what is distinctive about them. And the idea that only humans possess these sorts of more positive characteristics is difficult to sustain.

To begin with, there is the vast wealth of empirical evidence that suggests – to all but the most closed-minded behaviourist – that all social mammals are capable of deep feelings of affection towards each other. When wolves or coyotes reunite, after time spent apart hunting, they gallop towards each other at full tilt, yipping and whining, their tails wagging furiously. When they meet, they lick each other's muzzles and roll over with their legs flailing. African wild dogs are equally effusive: their greeting ceremonies involve cacophonies of squealing, dervish-like wagging of tails and extravagant leaps and bounds. When elephants reunite, they flap their ears, spin around and emit a deep greeting rumble. In all cases, unless you find yourself in the grip of an indefensible behaviourist ideology – an ideology that you insist on applying to other animals but refuse to apply to humans – the obvious conclusion is that these animals have genuine affection for each other, that they enjoy each other's company and that they are happy to see each other again.

Evidence of grief is equally compelling, and the more field studies are conducted the more compelling it becomes. Here, in his book *Minding Animals*, is Marc Bekoff describing an event in the life of a coyote pack that he studied in the Grand Teton National Park:

> One day Mom left the pack and never again returned. She had disappeared. The pack waited impatiently for days and days. Some coyotes paced nervously about, as if they were expectant parents, whereas others went off on short trips only to return empty-handed. They traveled in the direction she might have gone, sniffed in places she might have visited, and howled as if calling her home. For more than a week some spark seemed to be gone. Her family missed her. I think the coyotes would have cried if they could.

Foxes have been observed burying their dead mates. Three male elephants were observed standing over the de-tusked corpse of an older female who had been killed by poachers – they stood there for three days, touching her and trying to get her to stand up. The famous naturalist Ernest Thompson Seton once used the grief that a male wolf, Lobo, felt for the loss of his mate to trap and kill him. Seton, a wolf hunter before he became a writer, spread the scent of Lobo's mate, Blanca, by dragging her body across trap lines. Lobo returned to his beloved mate, only to be killed by Seton.

These are just anecdotes, you might say. Perhaps, but the anecdotes now number in their thousands and are growing every day – and that is ignoring the stories pet owners have to tell about their companions. Also, as Bekoff puts it, once you have enough anecdotes, they become something quite different: they become data. On any reasonable construal of 'enough', that transition point has long since passed.

One has only to read the wonderful work of Jane Goodall to understand that feelings of affection, empathy, even love are common in apes. And when, for example, she describes in *Through a Window* the rapid and painful decline of the young chimpanzee Flint following the death of his mother, Flo, one cannot, if one has even half a heart, fail to be moved. But evidence for the existence of these sorts of emotions in other mammals is just as strong. Affection, empathy and love – far from being uniquely human traits, or even uniquely simian traits, these are common throughout the world of social mammals.

There are, in fact, good theoretical reasons why this is so; reasons first adduced by Charles Darwin. Any social group needs something to bind it together – a form of social glue. For the social insects, the glue consists in both the pheromones that the insects use to communicate with each other and the fact that each social insect is more like an individual cell than an individual organism – a cell whose welfare and even identity is bound up with the hive or colony organism. But with mammals, evolution apparently employed a very different strategy that involved the development of what Darwin called the 'social sentiments': feelings of affection, empathy, even love. What holds together a wolf pack, or a coyote pack, or a pack of African hunting dogs is the same as what holds together a chimpanzee colony or a human family. This is what we all have in common.

I am, however, interested not in what we all have in common but in what distinguishes us from other creatures. And most of us accept – indeed insist – that it is our much-vaunted intelligence that separates us from 'dumb brutes'. If so, then we have to realize that this intelligence did not come for free. It came because, many ages ago, our ancestors walked a path that other social animals did not, and that path was paved with duplicity and conspiracy.

6

This general account of human intelligence is not seriously in doubt. In *Chimpanzee Politics*, Frans de Waal describes his classic study of the Arnhem chimpanzee colony and so demonstrates some of the complexities of chimpanzee group dynamics. In the colony, three males were continually vying for group leadership. At the beginning of the study, the alpha position was occupied by Yeroen. One of the important factors preserving his leadership was the support of the colony's female chimpanzees. Luit's protracted and ultimately successful bid to dethrone Yeroen was based on eroding this support. Prior to this challenge, Luit had occupied a relatively peripheral position in the colony – being forced by Yeroen to live slightly apart from the rest of the group. The key change in the dynamic occurred when another younger male, Nikkie, had grown up sufficiently to form an alliance with Luit. Together, the two of them engaged in a policy of 'punishing' – i.e. meting out beatings – to the females, not for the sake of it but with the aim of demonstrating Yeroen's inability to protect them. After around four months of the prosecution of this policy, the females started to support Luit, almost certainly because they were fed up with the punishment they were continually receiving from the pair and because of Yeroen's inability to prevent this.

Following his ascension, Luit quickly changed his policy. As leader, he now needed to change his attitude with respect to both the females and the other males. With the former, he relied on their general support and therefore adopted an even-handed keeper of the peace role. With the males, however, he became a loser-supporter. That is, when he intervened in a conflict between two males, it was usually to support the loser. Thus, even though his rise to leader had been secured with the help of Nikkie, he would routinely side with other apes in their disputes with Nikkie. This policy made good sense. A winner in a conflict between two males might be strong enough to directly challenge Luit's authority. But this would not be true of a loser. And by supporting the loser Luit also increased the probability of the loser's support in further conflicts. In other words, the exigencies of leadership required him to form alliances with those who could not challenge his authority to protect himself from those who could.

Eventually, Yeroen and Nikkie formed an alliance and deposed Luit. Nikkie became the new formal leader, but the real power seemed to belong to Yeroen. Indeed, following Nikkie's rise to the top, Yeroen worked so effectively against him that it is doubtful if Nikkie was ever really in control. Nikkie foolishly pursued a policy of supporting the winners in conflicts, and the peace was kept by Yeroen. For example, when Nikkie prepared to intervene in a conflict between two females, Yeroen would often turn on him and, perhaps aided by the two females, chase him away. Why did Nikkie put up with this? He had no choice: he needed Yeroen in order to keep Luit in check. Thus Nikkie was a leader who was never accepted by the females. Indeed, he was regularly set upon by alliances of them. Yeroen, on the other hand, formed alliances with the females in order to keep up the pressure on Nikkie, and formed an alliance with Nikkie in order to keep Luit in check. It is fairly clear who possessed the real power.

Yeroen's superior intelligence, relative to both Luit and Nikkie, consisted in his ability to form multiple alliances for multiple purposes: one alliance to keep Nikkie in check, another to keep Luit in check. Luit's alliance with Nikkie, in comparison, seems crude. To be a truly successful ape – to exhibit simian intelligence at its best – one must be able to conspire not just against one ape but against many. And the most successful apes are those who are able to conspire with the very same apes that they also conspire against.

In addition to the sort of scheming exhibited by Yeroen and Luit, the scheming that manifests itself in unstable and constantly shifting alliances, deception plays a pivotal role in all the classic studies of ape behaviour. Indeed, in an influential study ('The manipulation of attention in primate tactical deception', published in their volume *Machiavellian Intelligence*), Whiten and Byrne have distinguished no fewer than thirteen different types of deception commonly employed by apes. We don't need to worry about the details of each type; some representative examples will provide enough of a flavour.

A subordinate male chimpanzee or baboon will often hide its erect penis from a superior male – at the same time as it is deliberately displaying it to a female. To this end, it rests the arm that is closest to the dominant male on its knee and allows its hand to hang loosely down. All this time, it is shooting furtive glances at the other male. I think I love this example because it is so deliciously sleazy: only in apes do we find this inimitable combination of slyness and lasciviousness. This is a form of deception that Whiten and Byrne refer to as concealment. A common result of this episode of concealment is another: this time the male and female hide their entire bodies behind a convenient rock or tree and surreptitiously copulate.

Here is an example of a different type of concealment, one that Whiten and Byrne call inhibition of attending. A troop of baboons is travelling along a narrow trail. One baboon, female S, spots a nearly obscured clump of *Loranthus* – a vine that is highly prized by the baboon palate – in one of the trees. Without looking at the others, S sits down at the side of the trail and begins intently self-grooming. The others pass her by and, when they are out of sight, she leaps up into the tree and eats the vine. This is the baboon equivalent of pretending you have to tie your shoelace when you have, in fact, spotted a twenty-pound note lying on the ground.

7

It is easy to understand the connection between alliance-formation and deception on the one hand and increase in intelligence on the other. Both forms of behaviour require the ability to understand not just the world but also, crucially, the mind of another. Underlying both is the ability to see, understand or predict how the world appears for someone else.

Consider our sleazy chimpanzee, hiding his penis from the dominant male while displaying it to a female. To do this, the chimp must have a concept of the dominant chimp's perspective. That is, he must understand that the dominant chimp can see, that what he can see is not necessarily the same as what other chimps can see, and that what he can see is dependent on where he is in relation to other chimps. That is, to successfully engage in concealment, a chimp must have at least some idea of what is going on in the mind of other chimps. When primatologists talk of the impressive 'mind-reading' abilities of apes, they are talking about this ability.

The sophistication of mind-reading abilities is increased a notch or two in our second example of deception. In order to inhibit her attending or looking, the baboon S must not only have the idea that others might see the *Loranthus* vine, she must also have the idea that others might see her looking at the vine. That is, S understands that others might understand that she sees something significant in the tree. When S sees the vine, this is what is known as first-order representation: S has formed a visual representation of the world. If one of her companions understands that S is seeing something interesting, then it has formed a representation of her representation of the world. This is what's known as a second-order representation: a representation of a representation. However, when S understands that others might understand that she has seen something interesting, this is a representation of a representation of a representation: a third-order representation.

Here, again courtesy of Whiten and Byrne, is an even more impressive case. A chimp – let us call him chimp 1 – is going to be fed bananas. These are contained in a metal box that is opened from a distance. As the box is opening, another chimp – chimp 2 – appears. Chimp 1 quickly closes the metal box and walks away, sitting down a few yards away. Chimp 2 vacates the immediate area, but then hides behind a tree and watches chimp 1. As soon as chimp 1 opens the box, chimp 2 charges and relieves chimp 1 of the bananas. Chimp 1 can see that chimp 2 can see him seeing – this is third-order representation – but chimp 2 can see that chimp 1 can see that he can see him seeing. This appears to be a truly remarkable case of fourth-order representation.

The same sort of ability to understand the minds of others can also easily be seen when apes form alliances with and against each other. The key to any successful alliance – even a simple one – is to understand not only how your actions will affect others; equally importantly, it is to understand what sort of response your actions will prompt in others. That is, you must understand the relationship between what you do and what others will do because of what you do – recall Luit and Nikkie's campaign of violence against the female colony members. And to understand this is to understand how what you do provides reasons for what others do. To this extent, successful formation of even simple alliances involves understanding the minds of your fellow apes.

In short, the augmentation of intelligence that we find in apes and monkeys, but apparently not in other social creatures, is the result of twin imperatives: to scheme more than you are being schemed against and to lie more than you are being lied to. The nature of simian intelligence is irredeemably shaped by these imperatives. We became more intelligent so that we could better understand the minds of our peers, and so deceive them and use them for our own purposes – precisely what they were trying to do to us, of course. Everything else – our impressive understanding of the natural world, our intellectual and artistic creativity – came afterwards and as a consequence.

8

So far, however, we have left the most interesting question unanswered. Indeed, we have left the most interesting question unasked. Why would wolves have ignored the path to intelligence taken so effectively by apes? At this point, the experts shrug. Some have suggested that it might have something to do with group size. But this is little more than a vague gesture in the direction of an answer, since no one has ever made clear the connection between group size and the desirability of schemes and deception. I have another idea: a hypothesis that worms its way out, diffidently but nonetheless perceptibly, from either side of just about every line ever written in the literature on apes.

Luit is making advances to a female chimp, while Nikkie, who is at this time the official alpha male, is lying in the grass about fifty yards away. You can probably predict Luit's flirtation technique: he is flashing the female, displaying his erect penis while keeping his back towards Nikkie, so that he can't see what is going on. Nikkie, suspicions aroused, gets to his feet. Luit slowly shifts a few paces away from the female and sits down, once again with his back to Nikkie. He doesn't want Nikkie to think that he is moving only because he has spotted Nikkie's advance. Nonetheless, Nikkie moves slowly towards Luit, picking up a heavy stone on his way. Luit occasionally looks around to track Nikkie's progress, and then he looks back down at his penis, which is gradually losing its erection. Only when his penis is flaccid does Luit turn around and walk towards Nikkie. And then, in an impressive demonstration of just what a ballsy chimp he is, he sniffs at the stone before wandering off to leave Nikkie alone with the female.

Why did we walk an evolutionary path neglected by the wolf? Passages like this – and there are many of them – provide us with an unequivocal answer: *sex* and *violence*. This is what made us the men and women we are today. Even a lucky wolf – an alpha male or female – gets to have sex only once or twice a year. Many wolves never have sex – nor do they give any obvious signs of missing it or resenting their enforced abstinence. Ape that I am, I can't quite manage to look at sexual matters objectively; but imagine an ethologist from Mars engaged in a comparative study of the sexual lives of wolves and humans. Might not the ethologist conclude that the wolf's attitude towards sex is, in many ways, a fundamentally wholesome and restrained one: they enjoy it when they have it, but don't miss it when they don't? If we replaced the wolf with a human and sex with alcohol, we might say that the human had managed to cultivate a healthy attitude, steering effectively between the vices of excessive indulgence and repressive abstinence. But we can't bring ourselves to think about sex in this way. Of course we should miss it when we don't have it, we are compelled to think: this is natural, this is healthy. We think this way because we are apes. In comparison with the wolf, the ape is addicted to sex.

It is an interesting question why this should be. Perhaps it is simply that wolves don't know what they are missing. At least, that is what the ape in me wants to think. Female wolves are in reproductive cycle only once a year. The entire cycle lasts around three weeks and the wolf is fertile only during the middle week. In any pack, it is usually only the alpha female who will go into reproductive mode. The reasons for this are not understood. Some researchers suggest that it is a form of social stress occasioned by their status that prevents subordinate females from going into reproductive cycle. But this is more a guess than anything else.

Apes, on the other hand, typically do know what they're missing. Poor old youthful Brenin: with his misguided and perpetually thwarted attempts to copulate with every female dog in Tuscaloosa County; in his refusal to discriminate on the basis of breed or size; and in his utter contempt for the constraints imposed by simple physical possibility. He hadn't yet mastered the healthy and restrained attitude towards sex lauded by our imagined Martian ethologist. He must have had the idea that he was missing something – or else what was the point of all that effort? But, due to my constant vigilance, he wasn't in a position to know precisely what; nor would he be for many years to come.

Once you do know what you're missing, of course, then you will come to separate sex from reproduction in a way that Brenin was not able to do. Brenin was motivated by a blind genetic stirring, not by knowledge of the pleasure that would thereby follow – for he was unacquainted with that. But we apes know all about the pleasure. For the wolf, pleasure is a consequence of the drive to reproduce. The ape has inverted this relationship. For it, reproduction is an occasional – sometimes inconvenient – consequence of the drive to acquire pleasure. There is, of course, nothing wrong with this simian inversion. Different species embody different conceptions of the relation between reproduction and pleasure. But neither is there necessarily anything right with it.

The simian inversion does, however, have one clear consequence. The motivation to scheme and deceive will be far greater for apes than for wolves. Schemes and deception are the means the ape employs to satisfy the craving that goes with the simian inversion. This is not to say that they cannot scheme and deceive for purposes other than sex. Earlier, we saw how baboon S employed deception in order to acquire a tasty clump of *Loranthus*. However, we are trying to understand the respect in which apes are different from wolves. A wolf can be just as attracted to a hidden cache of food as an ape – but, unlike the ape, it will not try to acquire this through deception. The conclusion seems to be, therefore, that the ape's capacities for deception were acquired in a different context and for a different reason. The context and reason, I suggest, are, in part, provided by the simian inversion of pleasure and reproductive success.

The history of human thought – and not just Western thought – is organized around a distinction between rationality or intelligence on the one hand and pleasure or enjoyment on the other. The latter two are consigned to the realm of base or brute desires. It is our intelligence or rationality that makes us human and divides us from the rest of nature. I think, however, that rationality and pleasure are far more intimately connected than we have been willing to allow. Our rationality is, in part, a consequence of our drive to acquire pleasure.

Just as the motivations to scheme and deceive are greater for the ape, so too are the risks. Nikkie wasn't going to gently reprimand Luit: he picked up a heavy stone in order to pummel him more viciously than his bare hands would allow. What is often passed over in discussion of the impressive schemes and deceptions of apes is a certain kind of malice in the methods they employ to prosecute those schemes. This malice has no echo in the lives of wolves.

The fight between Brenin and Rugger was an impulsive and impromptu eruption. This is not to say that they wouldn't have killed each other given the chance. I don't know, not with any certainty, whether the fight would have resulted in death if allowed to continue – but if it had, it wouldn't have surprised me. However, had death been a consequence of the fight, there is no real sense in which it was an intended outcome. Brenin and Rugger simply lost their tempers. Their trespasses against each other were crimes of hot blood; they were crimes of passion.

Suppose Brenin and Rugger, Nikkie and Luit were humans. How would they fare in a court of law? Brenin and Rugger would have been condemned for losing their tempers. And if Nikkie had simply flown into a rage at the sight of Luit working his magic on a female and attacked him on the spot, that would have aroused similar condemnation. But Nikkie paused on his way over to Luit to pick up a rock. If Nikkie had gone on to attack Luit – and any clear sign of indiscretion on Luit's part would unquestionably have been enough for him to do this – then he would, and should, be judged more harshly for his assault. Picking up the rock proves intention; it is sufficient, under the law, to demonstrate premeditation. Nikkie's crime would have been one of cold blood, not hot blood. Given a reasonably sympathetic judge, the victor in the fight between Brenin and Rugger, if the fight had resulted in death, would have been convicted of manslaughter. But Nikkie, stone in hand, motivated by malice aforethought, would have been sent down for murder. I think this is what the difference between the malice of wolves and the malice of apes basically amounts to: the difference between manslaughter and murder.

Malice aforethought saturates so many simian interactions that one cannot help but conclude it is an endemic feature of the simian character. In fact, perhaps the single greatest contribution apes have made to the world – the single defining contribution for which they will always be remembered – is the invention of malice aforethought. If the reversal of the relation between reproduction and pleasure is the simian inversion, then we might call malice aforethought the simian invention.

Schemes and deception become so much more important when you are faced with a creature capable of malice aforethought. Put yourself in Luit's position, with Nikkie advancing on him, weapon in hand. If Luit had been a wolf, things would have gone much easier for him. The dominant male might have attacked, but Luit could easily have avoided serious punishment simply by submitting. But if Nikkie had been unconvinced by Luit's deceptions, then he would have beaten Luit mercilessly, come what may. No matter how abject his apologies, and no matter how sincere his expressions of remorse, the outcome was going to be the same. A wolf will quickly forgive and forget. But an ape is driven by malice aforethought and is not so easily mollified. The ape is merciless to its peers in a way that the wolf is not and could never be.

The eighteenth-century Prussian philosopher Immanuel Kant once wrote, 'Two things never cease to fill me with wonder: the starry skies above me and the moral law within me.' Kant was hardly atypical. An examination of the history of human thought shows that we value two things over all others. We value our intelligence: the intelligence that allows us to understand, among other things, the workings of the starry sky above us. And we value our moral sense: our sense of right and wrong, of what is good and what is bad; the sense that reveals to us the content of the moral law. Our intelligence and our morality, we think, distinguish us from all other animals. We are right.

However, rationality and morality do not come fully formed like Aphrodite from the waves. Our rationality is both impressive and unique; but it is also a superstructure erected on a foundation of violence and the drive to acquire pleasure. In Nikkie also we find, in nascent form, the vaguest intimations of a moral sense: a primitive sense of justice. Luit avoided a serious beating because Nikkie could not find sufficient grounds for acting against him. But it is no accident that a sense of justice should first come to be embodied in an ape. When one ape attacks another, and this attack is carried out with malice aforethought, and cannot be deflected by ritual gestures of conciliation on the part of the victim, then it is important that these attacks do not occur too often. If they do, then the colony will soon disintegrate. And so, because of its malicious and violent character, we find in the ape at least the beginnings of a type of sensitivity. There is a part of Nikkie which recognizes, albeit vaguely, that an attack on Luit must have grounds, where these are supplied by the presence of the appropriate evidence. This evidence provides his attack with justification and so makes it warranted. Grounds, evidence; justification, warrant: only a truly nasty animal would have need of these concepts. The more unpleasant the animal, the more vicious it is, and the more insensitive to the possibility of conciliation, the more it has need of a sense of justice. Standing on its own, alone in all of nature, we find the ape: the only animal sufficiently unpleasant to become a moral animal.

What is best about us comes from what is worst. That's not necessarily a bad thing. But it is something we might want to bear in mind.

4

Beauty and the Beast

1

When Brenin was a young wolf, his favourite game was to steal cushions off the sofa or the armchair. If I was in another room, perhaps working in my study, he would appear at the door, cushion in mouth, and, when he knew I had seen him, he would tear off through the house, through the living room, the kitchen and then out into the garden, with me in hot pursuit. The game was one of chase and could go on for quite a while. I had already covered dropping things in training – that was one function of the 'Out!' command – so I could have ordered him to drop the cushion at any time. But I didn't have the heart; and, anyway, the game was much more fun. And so he would charge around the garden, ears back, tail tucked low and eyes shining with excitement, while I thundered around ineffectively behind him. Until he was about three months old, Brenin was quite easy to catch – and so I just pretended he was too quick for me. But the pretence gradually shaded into reality. Soon he was throwing me little shimmies – feinting to go one way while actually going the other. When I caught on to this trick, the shimmies would become double shimmies. Eventually the game was played in a confused blur of feint, double feint and triple feint – feints nested within feints. When he was in the zone, when he had his game face on, I'm pretty sure Brenin had no idea what he was going to do next. And so, obviously, I didn't have clue. Of course, this sidestepping practice worked wonders for my rugby skills. I had always based my game on the idea of running over people rather than around them: I was what's known as a bosher. This worked well in the UK, but not as well in the US, where the people are generally much bigger and have been raised playing American football, where the tackling is ferocious. They are, however, much easier to confuse and, with all this instruction from Brenin, I became a twinkle-toed, sidestepping demon of the south-eastern United States.

My failure to catch Brenin bred a certain cockiness that he expressed in an early innovation to the game. After I was suitably exhausted, he would stand facing me and drop the cushion midway between us. 'Go on,' was the message. 'Take it!' As soon as I bent over to pick it up, he would leap in, seize the cushion and the chase would begin all over again. No matter how quick I became at bending and seizing the cushion, Brenin was always just a little bit quicker. It was a useful transferable skill: he once played the same game with a freshly cooked chicken that he had stolen from the kitchen during a momentary lapse of concentration on my part. I could have made him drop it, of course. But what was the point? I really didn't fancy the chicken after it had been in his mouth and so we played the game of chase.

Some professional animal trainers would regard our game with horror. I know this because they have told me so. Their objection was twofold. First of all, the game by its nature was likely to make Brenin more excitable – not a characteristic you want to encourage in a wolf. Secondly, my failure to catch Brenin might have led him to the conclusion that he was physically superior to me, and therefore caused him to bid for alpha status. Maybe these were legitimate worries; but with Brenin they never materialized. And this, I think, is because the games always proceeded according to a well-defined ritual that had a clear beginning and end. If I was in the living room, I would never allow Brenin to take the cushions. His attempts to do so were met with a firm, 'Out!' This told him that the game was something that could only be played at certain times. And the games always came to a definitive conclusion. I would say, 'OK, that's it!' Then I would make him bring the cushion to me and drop it. Then we would go inside and I would give him a treat of some sort, which both reinforced the end of the game and made him associate this ending with something good.

This all worked well for a while. However, when he got to be around nine months old, he decided to take the game to the next level. One morning, while I was writing in the study, I heard a succession of loud thuds from the living room. Not content with taking the cushions into the garden, Brenin had decided it might be a good idea to take the armchair too. And the thuds were caused by his repeatedly banging the chair against the door frame as he tried to drag it through. It was then that I realized a more radical approach towards Brenin's entertainment was required, an approach based on the premise that, all things considered, it would be best for both of us if Brenin were constantly exhausted. And so we began running together.

2

Trying to keep a wolf under control by making sure it's constantly exhausted is one approach. But even a moment's thought will tell you that it's not a very good one. Admittedly, our runs did tire Brenin out initially. Me too – but that was of lesser importance, since I wasn't the one trying to drag the furniture out into the garden. Brenin, on the other hand, became fitter and fitter, and therefore more capable of wreaking havoc on the house and its contents at any given time. Soon runs that used to plunge him into an exhausted slumber for the rest of the day he came to regard as a gentle *loosener*. And so the runs, of necessity, became longer and longer. But, of course, Brenin just got even fitter; and you can probably see where this is going. Bicycles were an option. But folks didn't take kindly to bicycles in Alabama back in those days – a fact I discovered through a near-decapitation incident involving me on a bicycle and some liquored-up rednecks with a baseball bat and a pick-up truck. Only pinko, commie, hippie bedwetters travelled under their own propulsion in Alabama back in those days. And so the bicycle option wasn't one I was really keen to explore at that juncture.

And so I kept running, and Brenin kept running with me; and we both got fitter, and leaner, and harder. This pragmatic impetus for my new-found fitness, however, quickly changed into something else. On our runs together, I realized something both humbling and profound: I was in the presence of a creature that was, in most important respects, unquestionably, demonstrably, irredeemably and categorically superior to me. This was a watershed moment in my life. I'm a confident guy. If people don't think of me as arrogant – perhaps they do – that's only because I'm good at hiding it. I can't ever remember feeling this way in the presence of a human being. That's not me at all. But now I realized that I wanted to be less like me and more like Brenin.

My realization was fundamentally an aesthetic one. When we were running, Brenin would glide across the ground with an elegance and economy of movement I have never seen in a dog. When a dog trots, no matter how refined and efficient its gait, there is always a small vertical vector present in the movement of its feet. If you have a dog, watch it closely the next time you take it out. As its feet go forwards, they also move up and down, no matter how slightly. And this movement of the feet will transmit itself to the line of its shoulders and back – if you watch, you will see them bob up and down as your dog travels forward. Depending on the type of dog you have, this movement will be obvious or almost indiscernible. But it's always there if you look carefully enough. With Brenin, you could see no such movement. A wolf uses its ankles and large feet to propel it forwards. As a result, there's far less movement in its legs – these remain straight, and move forwards and backwards but not up and down. So, when Brenin trotted, his shoulders and back remained flat and level. From a distance it looked as if he was floating an inch or two above the ground. When he was especially happy, or pleased with himself, this would be converted into an exaggerated bounce. But his default motion was the glide. Brenin is gone now, and when I try to picture him it is difficult to furnish this picture with the details necessary to make it a concrete and living representation. But his essence is still there for me. I can still see it: the ghostly wolf in the early-morning Alabama mist, gliding effortlessly over the ground, silent, fluid and serene.

The contrast with the noisy, puffing and leaden-footed thudding of the ape that ran beside him could not have been more pronounced or depressing. I wanted to be able to lope. I wanted to glide across the ground as if I was floating an inch or two above it. But no matter how good at running I became – and I became very good – this was always going to escape me. Aristotle once distinguished the souls of plants from those of animals. Plants, he claimed, have merely a nutritive soul – a soul whose function is to take in, process and excrete food. But the souls of animals, Aristotle called locomotive souls. It is no accident, I think, that he character- ized the souls of animals in terms of movement. Contrary to what I was told as a student, I don't think Aristotle simply meant that animals move around whereas plants do not. He was not, in general, a fan of platitudes. Rather, I think, if you want to understand the soul of the wolf – the essence of the wolf, what the wolf is all about – then you should look at the way the wolf moves. And the crabbed and graceless bustling of the ape, I came to realize with sadness and regret, is an expression of the crabbed and graceless soul that lies beneath.

Despite this rather unfortunate case of species-envy, my physical transformation continued apace. By the time he was a year old, Brenin stood thirty-four inches at the shoulder and weighed 120 pounds. When he was fully grown, he would add an inch and another thirty pounds to this. He was incredibly strong. And so I had to become stronger. On the one hand, I couldn't afford to have him challenging for alpha status. And, on the other, I was responsible for keeping him in line around other dogs. Rugger-type incidents were rare largely because Brenin would do what I told him to do. And I intended to keep it that way. So, four or five times a week, I would leave Brenin with someone for a couple of hours and hit the gym and trained harder than I had ever trained in my life. And so, by the time Brenin was a year old, and I was twenty-seven, I stood at five feet nine – no change there since I was twelve – and weighed 200 pounds. My body fat ratio was 8 per cent. And I could bench-press 315 pounds.

I could also curl at least 120 pounds. I know this not because I did it in the gym but because of the method I used to employ in separating Brenin from dogs. Actual fights, as I said, were rare. But I got pretty good at predicting when a fight was about to kick off. Then I would grab Brenin on each side of his neck and lift him off the ground, holding his face up to mine. I would stare into his amber eyes and whisper, 'Do you want a piece of me, son?' This, of course, sounds horribly macho; and I suppose it was. If you go to the gym five days a week, week in week out, then there is going to be a lot of testosterone sloshing around in your system. But there was method as well as machismo. Wolf parents carry their cubs by their necks. When this happens, the cubs stop struggling and allow themselves to be carried. By picking him up in this way, I was reinforcing the fact that I was the daddy in the relationship and that he should similarly stop struggling. I think Brenin knew exactly what was going on: I was presenting him with a readily understood scenario and one that clearly entailed an end to whatever he might have had in mind. In fact, the method only worked with his active complicity. He was at least as tall as I was. So I could actually lift him off the ground only because, when I grabbed him by the neck and started to lift, he would curl his back legs up under him – like a rabbit being lifted out of a conjuror's hat.

3

One afternoon, during the long, hot and extremely humid Alabama summer, I decided to go for a run. I also decided, uncharacteristically, to leave Brenin behind. He had been a little off colour for the past couple of days and I didn't want to risk him in the heat and humidity. My decision was one with which Brenin vehemently disagreed and had made his displeasure known. I left him in the house with a girlfriend looking after him.

After an apparently short process of trial and error, Brenin managed to open the garden gate – basically by smashing it off its hinges – and charged off after me. Since we didn't have a set route – it would change from day to day – I presume he was following my scent. About ten minutes into my run, I heard a screeching of brakes following by a loud and sickening thud. I turned to see Brenin lying in the road, having been hit by a Chevrolet Blazer. A Blazer, for those of you who are not American, is an SUV. The European version is the Vauxhall/Opel Frontera. But the Blazer, being American, is bigger. It had passed me a moment ago travelling at, I would estimate, somewhere in the region of forty to fifty mph. Brenin lay in the road for a few heart-stopping seconds, howling, and then he picked himself up and ran off into the woods at the side of the road. It took me nearly an hour to find him. But when I did, he was largely OK. Jennifer, our vet, confirmed that there were a few cuts and bruises, but no broken bones. And in a day or so he was back to normal. In fact, the Chevy came off distinctly worse.

That Blazer would have killed me. But Brenin's physical scars healed in just a few days. And, psychologically, there didn't seem to be any scarring at all. The very next day, he was pestering me to take him running and he never showed any subsequent fear of the cars that would fly past him on the road. Brenin was a very tough and together animal, both physically and psychologically. I want you to bear this in mind when I tell you the next story.

We were out running again, but this time it was a few years in the future. We had moved to Ireland – specifically Cork – and were running together along the banks of the River Lee. Leaving Lee Valley Park behind us, we headed out into the fields of cows that lined the river. Most people think of cows as stolid and slow-witted creatures, their lives expended in a miasma of standing and chewing and staring. Brenin and I knew differently. Every now and then, when the sun is just right and the wind carries on it the promise of summer, they will forget what they are – what ten millennia of selective breeding have made them – and dance and sing out in their celebration of what it is to be alive on a day like today.

The cows seemed inordinately fond of Brenin; and he clearly returned the sentiment. On spring days like this, whenever they saw us, they would stampede up from the furthest corners of the fields, baying and braying out their greeting. I suspect it was because they had just had their calves forcibly removed from them – they were dairy cows – and probably mistook Brenin for one of their own, a prodigal young returned to the green, green grass of home. Perhaps Brenin thought they took him for a god: the god of cows. Whatever the reason, he would trot up to them, giving each one of them a lick on her big wet nose. He may have not liked other dogs, but he really was quite fond of cows.

There were electric fences in those fields to keep cows in. When we were on the return leg of the run, I grabbed hold of Brenin's collar, since I saw, up ahead, Paco, the big St Bernard. Brenin was still officially hostile to all large male dogs and I didn't fancy having to step in to separate those two. As I grabbed his collar, we ducked under one of the electric fences. My elbow brushed the fence and the shock passed through to Brenin. Brenin took off in an undignified manner more reminiscent of a scalded cat than the god of cows, scorching straight past a somewhat mystified Paco. And he didn't stop until he reached the car, a couple of miles away. He was there waiting for me when I eventually got back, anxious and breathless. We had gone on that same run most days, rain or shine, for the best part of a year. But he never went back again. He refused point blank, and his decision would remain unchanged no matter what form of begging, bribery or coercion I employed. That, apparently, is how horrible electricity is for wolves. That is how much they must hate it.

Perhaps you might think Brenin was just being a little histrionic. It was, after all, only a mild electric shock. If you are tempted to think this, just remember the Chevy Blazer. On balance, it seems that for Brenin a mild electric shock was a lot worse than being hit by an SUV.

4

If you want to see human evil in all its purity, ingenuity and freedom, you will find it in a *shuttlebox*. This is an instrument of torture invented by the Harvard psychologists R. Solomon, L. Kamin and L. Wynne. The box consists of two compartments separated by a barrier. The floor of each compartment is an electrified grid. Solomon and his collaborators would put a dog in one compartment and then give it an intense electric shock to its feet. Instinctively, the dog jumps over from one compartment to the other. They would then repeat this procedure again and again – several hundred times in a typical experiment. Each time, however, the jump is more and more difficult for the dog, because the experimenters are gradually making the barrier higher and higher. Eventually the dog cannot make the jump and falls to the electrified grid beneath it – a panting, spasming, screaming wreck. In a variation, the experimenters electrify the floor on both sides of the barrier. No matter where the dog jumps, it is going to be shocked. Nevertheless, because the pain of the shock is intense, the dog tries to escape, no matter how futile the attempt. And so the dog jumps from one electrified grid to the other. The researchers, when they wrote up the experiment, described the dog as giving a 'sharp anticipatory yip which turned into a yelp when he landed on the electrified grid'. The end result is the same. Exhausted, the dog lies on the floor urinating, defecating, yelping, trembling. After ten to twelve days of these sorts of trials, the dog ceases to resist the shock.

If they had been discovered doing this in the privacy of their own homes, Solomon, Kamin and Wynne would have been prosecuted, fined and probably banned from keeping pets for a period of five to ten years. They should have gone to jail. But because they did their work in a Harvard laboratory, they were, instead, rewarded with the dubious trappings of academic success: cushy lifestyle, generous salary, the adoration of their students and the jealousy of their peers. Torturing dogs made their careers and spawned an entire dynasty of imitators. These sorts of experiments continued for more than three decades. Their most famous imitator, Martin Seligman, was a recent president of the American Psychological Association. Seligman doesn't do this sort of thing any more. Happiness is his thing now. Of course, dogs don't get to figure in experiments that make them happy. It's only the nasty experiments that they're allowed to be in.

Why was this torture permitted? Why was it thought to constitute valuable research? The experiments were thought to establish the so-called 'learned helplessness' model of depression: the idea that depression is something that can be learned. For a while, psychologists took this to be a result of great importance. However, no human being ever actually benefited from these experiments. Eventually – after thirty years of dog and assorted other animal electrocutions – it was concluded that the model didn't really stand up to careful scrutiny.

In these experiments, I think we find an instructive distillation of human evil.

5

Evil has fallen on hard times lately. Not in the sense that there isn't much of it around – quite the contrary – but rather in the sense that many purportedly intelligent people are loath to admit its existence. This is because they think of evil as an outmoded relic of medieval times – a supernatural force, emanating from the Devil, who performs his diabolical work by insinuating evil into the hearts of men and women.

So today we tend to put evil inside inverted commas. Now, what we call 'evil' is either a medical issue – the result of some form of mental illness – or a social issue – the result of some or other societal malaise. This has two consequences. First, 'evil' is something that resides only at the margins of society, in the psychologically or socially disadvantaged. Second, evil is not really anyone's fault. When a person does what we might be tempted to call 'evil' things, they can't be held for responsible for what they do. Either they're mentally ill or their social circumstances gave them no chance. They may be medically or socially dysfunctional, but they're not morally evil. Evil is never what it appears to be; evil is always something else.

I think this is all wrong. The modern, and supposedly enlightened, conception of evil has missed something really important. It's not that I want to defend the medieval conception of evil as a supernatural force. But the two central contentions of the modern conception of evil – that it exists only at the margins of society and is not really anyone's fault – cannot, I think, be sustained. In its place, I am going to recommend to you an account of evil that is deceptively simple. First, evil consists in very bad things. Second, evil people are those who do very bad things because of a certain kind of failure on their part.

Let us begin by trying to understand how we came to be so suspicious of the idea of evil. The modern suspicion of evil is based on the thought that evil deeds require evil people; and evil people must act from evil motives. And if you have no control over your motives – because you are ill or socially maladapted – then you have no control over the deeds. This connection between evil deeds and evil motives is no accident. It goes back to a distinction originally made in the Middle Ages:

between 'moral' and 'natural' evil. Medieval philosophers like Aquinas noted that evil – which they thought of as pain, suffering and related phenomena – could be caused by two different sorts of thing: natural events and human agency. Earthquakes, floods, hurricanes, disease, droughts and so on can all cause severe and protracted suffering. Pain and suffering caused in this way they referred to as natural evil. This they distinguished from the pain and suffering caused by human agency – the evil that humans do. This they called moral evil. But the idea of agency – of acting – involves the notion of a motive or intention. An earthquake or flood has no motive. It does not act. It simply happens. Humans, on the other hand, can act: they can do things. But doing something, as opposed to merely having it happen to you, requires acting with a motive. Falling down the stairs isn't something you do – it's something that happens to you. Genuine acts require motives. Therefore, people have inferred (though it doesn't strictly follow) that an evil person is someone who acts from evil motives.

The result is a highly intellectualized concept of moral evil. A good example of this is provided by Colin McGinn, a friend and one of the best philosophers around, who understands moral evil as essentially a kind of *schadenfreude*: taking delight in the pain, suffering or misfortune of someone else (although, to be fair, I don't think McGinn intended this to be a general account of moral evil). This may seem like a good way of understanding evil. Surely it is evil to take delight in the pain, suffering or misfortune of someone else? And surely the sort of person who does this is as good an example as any of an evil person? Actually, however, I don't think this idea is going to work.

A young girl is the victim of long-term abuse as a child, being regularly raped by her father from a very young age.

Horrified, you might ask, as I once did, what her mother was doing in all of this. Didn't she realize what was happening? The girl's reply chilled me to the bone, and does even today when I think about it. When her father came home drunk, abusive and spoiling for a fight – a regular occurrence in her household – her mother would tell her to, as she put it, go in there and keep him quiet. Whenever I need to keep an image of human evil firmly in my mind, I just think of this woman telling her daughter to go in there and keep him quiet.

There are two acts of evil involved here: the repeated episodes of rape by the father and the active complicity of the mother. And it is not easy to see which is worse. The mother was a victim – certainly – but was she any less evil? She traded her daughter's body, innocence and almost certainly any prospect of future happiness to buy herself fleeting relief from her monster husband. Her evil was, we must assume, fuelled by her terror – and not by any delight she took in the suffering or misfortune of her daughter. But this doesn't change the fact that her actions were as evil as it is possible to imagine. Just think about that when you assume that victims cannot be evil. If the father and the mother were not both evil, it is difficult to imagine anyone who is.

However, in neither case can this evil be properly understood in terms of motives, at least not the sorts of motives thought decisive by McGinn. Who knows what her father's motives were? Perhaps he understood what he was doing was evil. Perhaps not. Suppose he didn't. Suppose he thought it was a perfectly natural aspect of family life – maybe because he grew up in similar circumstances. Perhaps he thought this was simply how things were done. Perhaps he thought it was his right, as a father who brought his daughter into the world, to have absolute dominion over her – the right of a creator over his creation. Perhaps he thought he was doing his daughter a favour – preparing her, in, of course, as nurturing a manner as possible, for her sexual life to come.

All I can say is: who cares what he thought? There is no need to speculate on his motives. Even if he thought he was doing nothing wrong – even if he thought he was doing right – that diminishes his evil not one bit. His actions are still among the most evil imaginable.

You can be evil – as was the mother – because you fail in your duties of protection, and whatever terror you feel here is irrelevant. You can be evil – as was the father in our wholly speculative reconstruction of his motives – because you are an irredeemably stupid man. But in neither case does your evil have anything to do in taking delight in the pain, suffering or misfortune of others. Deliberate malice has, I think, little to do with the essence of evil. This is not to say that such malice plays no role in the commission of evil acts. It clearly does so in some cases. My point is that these cases are comparatively rare.

Let's now flash forward a few years, at least in our imagination, from the suffering of the daughter to the judgement of the parents. Let's suppose the father and mother were eventually caught and punished – whether this punishment could ever be sufficient is a matter of dispute. I'm not sure what, in these circumstances, the daughter's emotional reaction would be. Probably a little mixed, I would expect. But suppose it wasn't. Suppose she was absolutely delighted. Moreover, suppose she wasn't delighted because she thought their lengthy prison term might rehabilitate them – finally they could get the help they needed. And suppose she wasn't delighted because now at least they couldn't do it to anyone else. Nor was she delighted because of the deterrent effect their sentencing might have on other paedophiles. Suppose she was delighted for a much simpler and more basic reason: vengeance.

Suppose she hoped her father would not just be punished by his loss of freedom. Suppose she hoped that he would find himself sharing a cell with a big guy with a penchant for sodomy and rape, and so get a 'taste of his own medicine'. Would this be an evil hope? Would she be an evil person for hoping it? I don't think so. I think her desire for vengeance may be regrettable. It may be evidence of permanent psychological scarring, leading to an inability to ever really move on with her life. Maybe. But the woman could hardly be said to be evil in these circumstances. Delighting in the misfortunes of evil people – when you have personally suffered at their hands – may not be a shining example of moral development and maturity. But it is a long way from being evil.

So, I think *schadenfreude* is neither a necessary nor a sufficient condition for being an evil person. It is not necessary because you can be evil even if you don't delight in the pain, suffering or misfortune of others. You can be evil, as was the mother, because you don't do your duty. And you can be evil, as was the father in our speculative and presumably counterfactual reconstruction of his motives, because you have fundamentally stupid beliefs. And *schadenfreude* is not sufficient for being an evil person. Taking delight in the pain of evil others, especially when you have suffered at their hands, does not automatically make you evil.

Many people would be appalled if I mentioned the Solomon, Kamin and Wynne experiments in the same breath as the abused girl – as if that in some way diminishes her suffering. But this reaction has no basis in logic. The cases parallel each other. Underlying both cases is the existence of very bad things – pain and suffering on a scale most of us would not be able to imagine. And these very bad things are the result of a certain kind of failure on the part of their perpetrators. The failure is ultimately a failure of duty; but there are two different sorts of duty involved.

On the one hand, there is a failure to do one's moral duty. The particular duty in question is to protect those who are defenceless against those who deem them inferior and therefore expendable. If this is not a basic moral obligation, it is difficult to imagine what is. The mother was guilty of this failure, and, in the circumstances in question, her undoubted terror of her husband may mitigate but cannot eradicate her culpability.

There is, however, another kind of duty involved: something that philosophers call epistemic duty. This is the duty to subject one's beliefs to the appropriate amount of critical scrutiny: to examine whether they are warranted by the available evidence and to at least attempt to ascertain whether or not there exists any countervailing evidence. Today we have scant regard for epistemic duty: so sparingly is it honoured that most people would not even regard it as a duty (and this, itself, is a failure of epistemic duty). In our – perhaps implausible – reconstruction of his motives, the father was guilty of this sort of failure.

We find similar failures in the case of Solomon, Kamin and Wynne and their numerous imitators. We find, of course, ridiculous, unwarranted beliefs: the belief, for example, that torturing dogs with electricity is going to reveal anything at all interesting about the nature of human depression – with its multifarious causes, aetiologies and syndromes. With them too we find derogation of moral duty: the moral duty to protect a defenceless sentient creature from the sort of suffering that most of us, thankfully, would be unable to imagine.

We humans fail to see the evil in the world because we are so distracted by shiny and twinkling motives that we don't notice the ugliness beneath them. To be distracted in this way is a uniquely human failing. Whenever we look closely at evil, in its various forms and guises, we will always find staring back at us failure of epistemic duty and failure of moral duty. Evil that is the result of explicit intentions to cause pain and suffering, and to enjoy doing so, is a rare exception.

This has one notable consequence: there are more evil acts and more evil people than we would care to imagine or admit. When we think of evil in terms of medical illness or social breakdown, then we assume that evil is exceptional: evil is something that resides at the margins of society. But, in fact, evil pervades society all the way in. It attaches to abusive fathers and complicit mothers. But it attaches no less to privileged and happy Harvard psychologists, supposed experts in the domain of mental health, who acted, we can suppose, only out of the best intentions towards humanity. I have committed evil actions; many of them. And so have you. Evil is quotidian; it is commonplace. It is banal.

In her brilliant discussion of the trial of Adolf Eichmann, Hannah Arendt introduces the idea of the banality of evil. Eichmann's crimes as the SS officer in charge of the Nazi regime's systematic extermination of Jews, she argued, stemmed not from his desire to inflict pain or degradation. He had no such desire. Rather, his evil actions stemmed, she argued, from his inability to empathize with his victims and his inability to subject his beliefs and values to the appropriate scrutiny. I agree with Arendt that evil is banal. But it is our unwillingness, rather than our inability, that makes it so. There was no general inability on the part of Solomon, Kamin and Wynne to examine their beliefs. They were just unwilling to do so. There was no inability on their part to protect those dogs from further torture. They were just unwilling to do so.

Immanuel Kant once said, correctly, that ought implies can. To say that you ought to do something implies that you are able to do it. Conversely, to say that you ought not do something – that you shouldn't do it – implies that you are able to not do it. When we understand the banality of evil in terms of inability, then it provides us with an all too convenient excuse: we couldn't have done things any differently from the way we in fact did. Inability takes away culpability. And we are not, I think, so easily excused.

A failure to do one's duty, both moral and epistemic, a failure grounded in unwillingness rather than inability, underwrites most of the evil in the world. However, there is one further ingredient of evil, without which neither failure is of any consequence: the helplessness of the victim.

6

You may have noticed that the general drift of this chapter does not sit entirely comfortably with the discussion of the uniqueness of apes in the previous one. There, I argued that one thing apes unquestionably bring to the world is a kind of malice aforethought that animates their dealings with each other. This would lead naturally to the idea that distinctively human evil is the result of deliberate malice. However, in this chapter I have argued that most of the evil produced by humans is not the result of malicious intentions, but of the unwillingness to do one's moral and epistemic duty. But we are only halfway through our account of evil and there is plenty of time for the simian invention to be brought into play. Deliberate malice does play a crucial role in human evil; not so much in the commission of acts, but in preparing the ground upon which those acts can be performed. The malice of apes – and human apes in particular – is to be found in their manufacture of helplessness. In this, human apes engineer the possibility of their own evil.

The dogs were as helpless as the daughter. Children are naturally helpless, but dogs have been manufactured to be that way. Solomon, Kamin and Wynne thought of themselves as studying the phenomenon of learned helplessness, and all the while they were complicit in the business of manufacturing helplessness. This may seem ironic, but there is no irony here, only intention. To study helplessness in humans they first had to manufacture it in an animal.

In his novel *The Unbearable Lightness of Being*, the Czech writer Milan Kundera says something that I think is fundamentally important and correct about the nature of human goodness:

> True human goodness can manifest itself, in all its purity and liberty, only in regard to those who have no power. The true moral test of humanity (the most radical, situated on a level so profound that it escapes our notice) lies in its relations to those who are at its mercy: the animals. And it is here that exists the fundamental failing of man, so fundamental that all others follow from it.

If we humans place such disproportionate weight on motives and if these are simply masks that hide an ugly truth beneath, then to understand human goodness we must strip away those motives. When the other person is powerless, you have no self-interested motive for treating them with decency or respect. They can neither help nor hinder you. You do not fear them, nor do you covet their assistance. In such a situation, the only motive you can have for treating them with decency and respect is a moral one: you treat them in this way because that is the right thing to do. And you do this because that is the sort of person you are.

I always judge a person by how they treat those who are weaker than them. I judge the rich diner by how he treats the waiters and waitresses that serve him. I judge the office manager by how he treats his workers. You find out much about a person from this. But even here the test is not absolutely accurate. The insulted waiter can spit, or worse, in the diner's soup. The office workers can do a poor job, thus getting the manager into trouble with his managers. You find out something important about a person when you see how they treat those who are weaker than them. But you find out most about a person when you see how they treat those who have absolutely no power; those who are helpless. And, as Kundera points out, the most obvious candidates for this status are animals.

Ironically enough, for a creature traditionally used to symbolize the dark side of the human soul, Brenin actually didn't come out too badly in terms of Kundera's test. His fights, though savage and bloody, always involved a dog who was big, aggressive and as violent as he was. In other words, they always involved a dog whom Brenin perceived as an actual or possible threat. I knew many of them; they were owned by my fellow rugby players or their associates. Some of these dogs would smash their heads through a pane of glass if they thought it would get them to a fight on the other side. They were, and this is a simple, objective truth, actual or potential threats. Dogs that were demonstrably weaker than him, he would treat either with indifference or with a peculiar sort of kindness. I remember a six-month-old male Labrador charging up to Brenin from afar, his owner running frantically behind him; the dog jumped all over Brenin in his excitement – and Brenin used to hate it when that happened. But there wasn't a thing he could do about it. In the end, he placed the Labrador's entire head in his mouth and gently held it there to try and restrain him. You should have seen the owner's face. Perhaps I'm being led astray by the rosy glow of nostalgia, but, as far as I can recall, if you judge Brenin by Kundera's test then I think he actually emerged with moral reputation reasonably intact.

Just as true human goodness can manifest itself only in relation to those who have no power, so too is weakness – at least relative weakness – a necessary condition of human evil. And it is here, I think, that we find the fundamental failing of human beings. Humans are the animals that manufacture weakness. We take wolves and we make them into dogs. We take buffalo and we make them into cows. We take stallions and we make them into geldings. We make things weak so that we may use them. In this, we are utterly unique in the animal kingdom. The abused child was naturally helpless. But Solomon, Kamin and Wynne's dogs were the product of 15,000 years of social and genetic engineering that led them, eventually but inexorably, to an electrified shuttlebox.

Humans are not unique in treating the weak or helpless

badly. All animals exploit the weak – although generally they have no choice in this. A pack of wolves will make numerous dummy attacks on a herd of caribou, precisely so that they may look for signs of weakness in one of the herd. When these signs are detected, they will focus their energies on that individual. A wolf mother will kill its cub if it perceives unusual signs of weakness in it. Life is a deeply unpleasant process that sifts the weak from the strong. Life is profoundly cruel.

What is characteristic of humans, however, is that they have taken the unkindness of life, refined it and thereby intensified it. They have taken life's cruelty to another level. If we wanted a one-sentence definition of humans, this would do: humans are the animals that engineer the possibility of their own evil.

It is no accident that we are these animals. In the ape, as we have seen, social intelligence comes first. We are so adept at manufacturing weakness in other animals because we were first able to do it to each other. The schemes and the lies of an ape are its attempt to make apes that are stronger than it weaker than it. The ape in us is always alive to the possibility of engineering weakness in other apes. It is always watching for an opportunity to practise evil.

The thing is, what goes around comes around. It is not possible to understand others as opportunities to be exploited, as bearers of weaknesses to be exposed, without this eventually turning back on you and decisively tainting the way you think about yourself. I implicitly understand myself as a bearer of weaknesses to be exposed because I have, all my life, understood others in this way. The weakness we manufacture in ourselves consists, fundamentally, in a certain way of thinking about ourselves and the evil acts we commit. We whine our excuses; we snivel of our extenuating circumstances. We couldn't have done otherwise, we tell ourselves and anyone else who will listen. Perhaps this is true. But our weakness consists in thinking that this matters. A wolf does not make excuses. A wolf does what it does – perhaps what it has to do – and accepts the consequences.

The idea that evil is a medical condition, or the result of social malaise, is ultimately because we have now engineered in ourselves the helplessness we have carefully constructed in others. We are no longer, we think, even worthy subjects of moral evaluation. If we are bad, or we are good, then this is really something else – something that must be explained in other, non-moral, terms; something beyond our control. To explain away our moral status, to excuse our own culpability in the manufacture of evil, this is the ultimate manifestation of that manufacture of evil – the clearest expression imaginable of the weakness that we have assiduously assembled in our own souls. To think of morality as really something else – the weakness is so palpable that only a human could miss it. We are no longer strong enough to live without excuses. We are no longer even strong enough to have the courage of our convictions.

7

The universe, we are told, began with a big bang. This was followed by rapid expansion – from an inconceivably small point of singularity to an inconceivably large, and continually expanding, cosmos. Eventually, this cosmos cooled enough for matter to form, resulting in the familiar dualism of today's universe – matter and space. This matter condensed further, forming discrete stars and, later, planets. On some planets – at least one that we know of, but presumably more – life began to form. Originally this consisted in simple organic molecules floating in a soup of even simpler con-stituents. But these molecules began to compete with one another for the soup's free atoms. The increasing complexity of one molecule was bought only with the stagnation or demise of others. From its very inception, life was a zero-sum game. Some molecules, therefore, became specialists at detecting weakness in the molecules around them. They became molecular carnivores, exploiting the weaknesses they discovered, breaking molecules down and appropriating their constituent atoms. And the process rumbled on and on, for billions of years, producing progressively more and more complex living molecules.

It's not that the universe had any say in this, of course: things just happened in it, as far as we know without any overall direction or control. But after around four billion years or so, something unexpected and rather impressive happened: the universe became capable of asking itself ques-tions. Tiny parts of the universe became capable of asking questions about themselves, about other parts of the universe and even about the universe as a whole. Eventually, one day during the early 1990s, two of the products of this process, one of whom was fond of such questions, found themselves out running together in the cool of an Alabama early-summer morning. And one little part of the universe, one that was puffing and thudding gracelessly through the streets of Tuscaloosa, was asking itself the question: was it worth it? After four billion years of blind and unthinking develop-ment, the universe had come to contain me. Was it worth it? And, a comparative question: after four billion years of blind and unthinking development, the universe had also come to contain Brenin. Who was more worth it?

Of the two of us, I was, I assume, the only one who could ask these questions. Does that make me a more worthwhile thing for the universe to have produced? Humans have typically thought so. According to Martin Heidegger, the twentieth-century German philosopher, the distinctiveness – and by extension the value – of a human consists in the fact that a human is a being whose being is an issue for it: that is, a human is the sort of creature that can ask questions such as, 'What am I?' and 'Was I worth it?' It is our rationality, broadly construed, that makes us better than other animals. But it is truly difficult to understand what this word 'better' means. I was better at working my way through complex logical or conceptual problems – at least on my good days, and after my first morning infusion of caffeine. But Brenin was better at running. Which of these skills is better?

One way, perhaps the most obvious way, of understanding the word 'better' would be as 'more useful'. But if so, 'better' is necessarily relative to the creature in question. What is useful for me is not necessarily what is useful for Brenin – and vice versa. It is useful for Brenin to be able to run quickly and change direction on a sixpence – that is how, at least in his ancestral home, he would be able to catch the things he needed to eat. For me, however, such skills are far less useful. Each animal brings with it its own form of life, and which skills are better or more useful are relative to that form of life.

The same is true when we try to understand 'better' in terms of the idea of excellence. Ambitious and subtly competitive ape that I am, I have always, I suppose, striven for excellence – well, maybe not always, but at least in the recent past. For me, excellence involves an ability to think through difficult conceptual problems and record the results of my ruminations on paper. According to a long tradition of thought, instigated by Plato, rationality is the distinctively human excellence. But this just reiterates that the idea of excellence is also relative to an animal's form of life. Excellence for the cheetah consists in speed, for speed is what the cheetah specializes in. Excellence for the wolf consists, among other things, in a certain sort of endurance that sees it able to run for twenty miles in pursuit of its prey. What is excellent depends on what you are.

Rationality is better than speed or endurance: that is what we find ourselves, perhaps irresistibly, tempted to say. But on what basis could we justify this claim? There is no objective sense of 'better' that would allow us to do so. Once we say this, the word 'better' loses its meaning. There is simply what is better for a human and what is better for a wolf. There is no common standard in terms of which the different senses of better may be judged.

We humans find this difficult to see because we find it so difficult to be objective about ourselves. And even I can't quite shake the suspicion that I must be missing something. So, here is an exercise in objectivity. Medieval philosophers used a phrase that I think is both beautiful and important: *sub specie aeternitatis* – under the gaze of eternity. Under the gaze of eternity, you see yourself as just one speck among others in the vast starry blackness of the universe. Under the gaze of eternity, we human beings are merely one species among others – a species that hasn't been around for very long, and gives every indication of not being around for too much longer. What does the gaze of eternity care for my ability to work my way through complex conceptual problems? Why should the gaze of eternity care for this any more than for Brenin's ability to glide over the ground as if he were floating an inch or two above it? The idea that the gaze of eternity cares any more for my ability is just a petty conceit.

If we cannot judge other animals – if there is no coherent content to the idea that we are objectively better than they are – then we can nonetheless admire them. And our admiration will be informed and guided by the realization, however murky, that they have something that we lack. Often, maybe even typically, what we admire most in others is what we find lacking in ourselves. So what was lacking in this ape that he should admire so much the wolf running beside him?

There was, of course, a certain sort of beauty that I couldn't possibly emulate. The wolf is art of the highest form and you cannot be in its presence without this lifting your spirits. No matter what sort of foul mood I was in when we began our daily run, bearing witness to that kind of silent, gliding beauty always made me feel better. It made me feel alive. More importantly, it is difficult to be around such beauty without wanting to be more like it.

But if the art of the wolf was something that I couldn't emulate, underlying it was something else: a strength that I could at least try to approximate. The ape that I am is a crabbed, graceless creature that deals in weakness; a weakness that it manufactures in others, and a weakness with which it is ultimately infected. It is this weakness that permits evil – moral evil – a foothold in the world. The art of the wolf is grounded in its strength.

When Brenin was around two months old, I took him to rugby practice, as usual. This was during the time that he had taken to tormenting Rugger and Rugger didn't like him at all. Eventually, Rugger lost his temper, grabbed Brenin by the neck and pinned him to the ground. To his great credit, that's all Rugger did. He could easily have snapped Brenin's little neck like a twig. Even a pit bull can pass Kundera's test. But it is Brenin's reaction that will always stay with me. Most puppies would have screeched out in shock and fear. Brenin growled. This was not the growl of a puppy, but a deep and calm and sonorous growl that belied his tender age. That is strength. And that is what I have always tried to carry around with me, and I hope I always will. As an ape, I will fall short of this; but I have an obligation, a moral obligation, never to forget it and to emulate it as far as I can. If I can only be as strong as a two-month-old wolf cub, then I am a soil where moral evil will not grow.

An ape would have scurried away to darkly plot his revenge; to work out ways of manufacturing weakness in those who are stronger than him and who have humiliated him. And when that work is complete, then evil can be done. I am an ape through accident of birth. But in my best moments I am a wolf cub snarling out my defiance to a pit bull that has smashed me into the ground. My growl is a recognition that pain is coming, for pain is the nature of life. It is the recognition that I am nothing more than a cub and, at any time, the pit bull of life can snap my neck like a twig. But it is also the will that I won't back down, no matter what.

I once had a colleague who was unusual among philosophers in that he was a believer. He always used to tell his students: when the shit hits the fan you will believe. Maybe that's what happens. When the shit hits the fan, people look for God. When the shit hits the fan, I remember a little wolf cub.

5

The Deceiver

1

There is a story of a wolf that lived in Gubbio, Italy, and his encounter with St Francis of Assisi. The wolf had been terrorizing the villagers and St Francis was asked to persuade him to desist. The wolf and the saint met one day outside the city walls and came to an agreement – a contract duly notarized by the city's appropriate official. The wolf agreed to stop terrorizing the townsfolk and to leave their cattle alone. The residents of Gubbio, in turn, promised to feed the wolf and allow him to wander at will through the town. This story amuses me, because I had come – quite independently – to pretty much the same arrangement with Brenin. Specifically, the version of the contract I had reached with the young Brenin went something like this:

OK, Brenin. I will take you everywhere I go: to my
lectures, to the rugby training after the lectures, and to
the matches at the weekend, whether they are home or
away. If I go shopping you can come too, but you'll
have to stay in the car (I'll be quick!). And, no, I won't
leave you in the car during the heat of the day, and it's
therefore lucky we have a twenty-four-hour
supermarket just down the road. I shall make sure you
have a long and interesting walk every day, and if I go
running, you can come too. You will have a good
nutritional meal every day. And when you turn in for
the night you will be suitably exhausted from yet
another wondrous day of enjoyment and novelty. And
here's another one – I don't realize it yet, but it will
become painfully apparent as the years wear on: every
house I ever buy will cost me at least fifty grand more
than it otherwise would have just because it must
have a decent-size garden for you to run around in.
You, on the other, have to not destroy that house.
That's all I ask really. Sometimes, I realize, you might
be uncontrollably tempted by a Hungry Man meal I
have imprudently left within your reach. Shit
happens. I'm not going to dwell on it, or give you a lot
of grief over that sort of thing. What I do ask is that
you leave the bloody house alone. That means no
destruction of items contained therein. And while I
understand that you are a young wolf and accidents
may sometimes happen, particularly at night, please
try not to pee on the carpets.

If you replace my house with the town of Gubbio and me
with St Francis, the two stories replicate each other almost

perfectly. But, unlike St Francis, I broke the contract – and even now, more than a decade later, it still bothers me.

Alabama was essentially a seven-year party. I've been fortunate in my life in many ways. And one of those ways was to have the opportunity to live, in all essentials (i.e. the parties, the drinking, the sport of various stripes), the life of an undergraduate twice. It was much more fun the second time around – perhaps because I had money this time. Or perhaps, just as youth is wasted on the young, the life of a student is wasted on students. Who knows?

Our wild days changed irrevocably when Brenin was four and I was thirty. The truth be told, we were probably both getting a little old for that life anyway. I was twenty-four when I first took up the job in Alabama. Living the life of a student when you are twenty-four is one thing, but there is only so long you can keep going to student rugby parties before it gets, first, a little sad and, after that, a little creepy. But the immediate cause of our move was not my increasing age but my father's. One bout of pneumonia followed another. Increasingly, I suspected that he was going to die – and thought that I should be closer to home. Of course, the old bastard actually made a full recovery. He's still around today. But by then it was too late: my days of keg parties and scantily clad rugger huggers were behind me.

But it was the best thing I ever did – even if it didn't seem like it at the time. I had unfinished business with philosophy. The dissolute but highly enjoyable life I was living in Alabama had resulted in my writing and publishing drying up completely. Clearly, I wasn't disciplined enough to ignore the obvious temptations of the life around me, so I had to change that life. Therefore, for my move back across the Atlantic, I decided to go somewhere really quiet. I needed somewhere out in the countryside for Brenin. And crucially, I needed a place where there was absolutely, positively nothing for me to do except write. So we moved to Ireland and I took up a job as college lecturer at University College Cork. Oh, and the other somewhat significant factor influencing my decision to go there: this was the only place desperate enough to actually offer me a job. That's what happens when you've been to a party for the last seven years.

The problem was that Brenin had to spend six months at the pleasure of the Irish government, at the Lissadell detention centre in Swords, just north of Dublin. These were the days before pet passports and Brenin had to go into quarantine for six months. This was an unspeakably stupid and evil system. It was devised before the invention of a rabies vaccine, and it took both Britain and Ireland the best part of a century to catch up with this 'recent' medical development. Brenin had been receiving annual rabies vaccinations since he was a cub and the antibodies were demonstrably present in his blood. Nevertheless, in common with thousands of other dogs in a similar situation, he had to do his time.

I don't know about Brenin, but this was the hardest thing I've ever had to do. And I spent many nights of those six months crying myself to sleep. I still don't know if I did the right thing by him: six months is a very long time in the life of a wolf. But one thing about Brenin that separated him from the average dog was that he was a very together animal. He always was — even as a cub. Nothing really fazed him. You've seen that already in his encounters with Rugger the pit bull. He could, I suspect, have done his time standing on his head. He in fact did it with aplomb, and without any of the obvious psychological difficulties that scar many dogs put in quarantine.

The Deceiver

It was actually a fairly soft regime in Lissadell. Majella, the governor, loved Brenin: quite understandably, since he was far and away the best-looking 'dog' ever to grace Ireland with its presence. He was, at this time, masquerading as a malamute – that's what I put on the import form – since the legal status of wolves in Ireland is dubious. Malamutes were at the time unknown in Ireland, and even the vets were not sure what they were supposed to look like. Because of his stunning good looks and his pleasant, courteous manner, Majella accorded him various privileges. The most important of these was the run of the entire facility for most of the morning. He used this time, apparently, to stamp his authority over the other inmates, largely in the form of urinating all over the front of their runs. I used to go up there once a week – in those days, a ten-hour round trip on those crappy Irish roads – and we would walk around the complex together for a few hours. His privileges were eventually curtailed after a surreptitious but nonetheless ill-advised rooting through Majella's shopping bag and rapid devouring of her frozen chicken. But, by then, he was nearly out anyway.

When he was released, I did my best to make things up to Brenin. This meant long runs every day. We spent the summer of his release – he was released in June – in west Wales, at my parents' house. Actually, it wasn't quite in their house. We had to live in the mobile home at the bottom of the garden, since Brenin had taken an immediate dislike to my parents' Great Danes, Bonnie and Blue. In fact, within a few hours of arriving he had tried to kill Blue on several different occasions. The days we spent running on, and near, the magnificent beaches of Freshwater West, Broadhaven South and, his favourite, Barafundle. There were a gazillion rabbits in the dunes behind Barafundle, and here Brenin started to learn something I could not, because of the snakes, let him do in Alabama: to hunt.

At the end of the summer, we moved over to Ireland. For our first year there, we lived in Bishopstown, a suburb on the western fringes of Cork City. I tried to make Brenin's life as much like Alabama as possible. So we would go running every day – usually to the Lee Valley Park and its adjoining fields. Or we would go to Powdermills Park in Ballincollig. At weekends, we would head out to various places: the beach at Inchydoney, Glengarra Woods up past Mitchelstown on the road to Dublin, the cliff walk at Ballycotton and many more. I started surfing around this time, and a couple of days a week, surf permitting, we would head down to windswept Garrettstown beach, where Brenin would splash around in the water while I tried to stand up on my board. Quarantine may have been tough, but this was a much better place for him than Alabama – and, thanks to St Patrick, we didn't have to worry about snakes.

2

The fact that something is inevitable does not necessarily make it any less unpleasant. I knew that I had to move back across the Atlantic. I knew that Brenin would have to go into quarantine. I knew that he would have a much better life over there, in a climate and countryside far better suited to him. But I still can't quite shake the horror of that day in early December when I drove him to Atlanta to put him on a plane. I still have a recurring nightmare about it, and I wake up to double crushing blows. Initially, I am sad because in my dream I am betraying Brenin. And then I remember he is dead. The story of St Francis and the wolf of Gubbio is a happy story about a contract with a wolf. It is a happy story because the contract is kept. But there is a far darker story of a wolf and a contract, a story about the dire consequences of breaking the contract.

Fenrisulfr was a giant wolf of Norse mythology. He grew up in unhappy filial circumstances. His brother, Jörmungandr, the Midgard serpent, was cast into the sea by Odin for no good reason, at least nothing that would stand up in court. His sister, Hel, was banished to the land of the dead merely on the word of a crone of dubious sanity but demonstrable malice. So, presumably the first lesson we should learn about the gods is a simple one: you can't trust them. And, indeed, it's not as if Fenrisulfr had ever given the gods any specific reason to distrust him. On the contrary, bearing in mind that he was a giant wolf whose rumoured destiny – on the day of Ragnarok, the end of the world – was to swallow the sun, he had hitherto led a life of the most remarkable restraint. But as he grew larger, the gods began to fear him, and their solution – characteristically devoid of imagination – was to chain him up and forget about him. First they made a chain called Loedingr. But that didn't hold him for long. Then they made Dromi, another iron chain, but twice as strong as Loedingr. He smashed through that one too. So then they had their dwarves fashion another chain. It was made from the sound of a cat's footfall, the beard of a woman, the roots of a mountain, the spirit of a bear, the breath of a fish and the spittle of a bird.

Here, then, is the second lesson we should learn about the gods – a lesson that, in a reasonably straightforward way, explains the first. It's not that the gods are particularly stupid, though some of them, let's face it, are not the sharpest knives in the drawer. Nor are they necessarily vicious and malignant, although many of them are. Rather, they are characterized by a certain incapacity to understand the minds of others. The gods have no theory of mind; they have a congenital inability to put themselves in the other person's shoes. They have no empathy. To put it bluntly, probably the safest characterization of the gods is that they are all sociopaths.

Did they really think that Fenrisulfr would fall for this? He had given no indication of being an especially unintelligent wolf. But they try him out on two chains, the heaviest and thickest iron chains ever forged. These don't work, so they present him with something that looks like a silk ribbon. And they don't think that he's going to realize something's up? So, Fenrisulfr called them on this. No, no, they assured him. There's no trick. On my mother's life, Odin is alleged to have said, perhaps thinking he was engaging in a subtle in-joke (which would merely confirm the vast body of textual evidence suggesting that subtlety was never Odin's forte).

At this point, the official version of events goes something like this. Tyr, the bravest of the gods, volunteered to put his hand in Fenrisulfr's mouth, as a gesture of good faith, thus nobly sacrificing his own appendage for the greater good. But mythology is, of course, written by the winners. Perhaps I have spent too much time with a wolf, but this official version of the story never did really ring true for me. Indeed, I think it bears all the hallmarks of a version subsequently invented and stubbornly championed by Tyr. One can't help suspect that Tyr was not the bravest but the most degenerately cruel and vicious of the gods. And given the widely acknowledged but largely unexplained interest he had taken in the raising of Fenrisulfr, it is, sadly, possible that much of Fenrisulfr's early life, from the time he was a cub, had been spent suffering, in one way or another, at the hands of Tyr. And, if so, Fenrisulfr would have put him high on his list of things to bite. One can't also help suspect that Tyr didn't volunteer to put his hand in the giant wolf's mouth. Rather, Odin ordered him to do so – on pain of severe and protracted suffering should he refuse. In which case, one can imagine the look on Tyr's face when he actually worked up the courage to do as Odin commanded, or rather worked up the courage to not resist the other gods forcing his hand in Fenrisulfr's mouth. Fenrisulfr gives Tyr a little wink and the bravest of the gods almost certainly proceeds to soil his breeches.

Perhaps Tyr's hand was worth it. Perhaps Fenrisulfr was quite willing to play the gods' game. It wasn't yet his time, nor would it be for many years. When his time did come, at Ragnarok, legend has it that he was so large that his upper jaw touched the sky while his lower one touched the earth. Still, that was a while off yet. And he was a very together wolf. He could do the time – he could do the time standing on his head. He, in fact, spent it chained to a rock called 'scream', on the island of Lyngvi. Of course, Tyr wanted revenge. So, not content with chaining Fenrisulfr until the end of time, for his pièce de résistance he drove a sword into the wolf's mouth. This caused slaver to run from his jaws and it formed a river. The river was called 'hope'. And the chain that bound Fenrisulfr until Ragnarok was called Gleipnir: the deceiver.

The tragedy of this story, of course, is that no one really knows how Fenrisulfr would have behaved had he not been treated in this appalling fashion. On the day of Ragnarok, he famously sided with the giants against the gods, taking his revenge on Odin by disembowelling him. But who knows what side he would have taken had the gods not reneged on their contract with him. And after they had broken this contract, what right did they have to even expect Fenrisulfr's support?

The horror of that drive to Atlanta lay not in the knowledge that I would miss Brenin so much. It lay in the fact that I did not know what side he would take when he got out. Would he be on the side of gods or giants? And what right did the gods – if I might modestly, and I assure you sarcastically, put it – have to expect his support after their betrayal?

In some versions of the myth, the gods understand the inevitability of their actions. They know that they have no choice in the binding of Fenrisulfr. They know that they must be defeated at Ragnarok – the time of the gods will have passed and must be replaced by an age of giants. They know that the chaining of Fenrisulfr and his taking the side of giants are required for their defeat. They know that what they do must be done. But to know that what you do is necessary does not release you from the crushing burden of actually doing it.

Saying goodbye to Brenin that day in Atlanta broke my heart because I didn't know if he – Brenin, my Buffalo Boy – would still be there when I saw him again; or whether he would have been replaced by another wolf living inside his pelt.

3

With hindsight, I suppose it's natural – and maybe depressingly predictable – for a philosopher to think of the formation of our little nation of two in contractual terms. The notion of a social contract has played a prominent role in the history of

Western thought. Its principal progenitor was a seventeenth-century English philosopher, Thomas Hobbes.

For Hobbes nature was unpleasant – red in tooth and claw (as Tennyson would later put it). Humans once lived in a state of nature, which basically meant a war of each against all. No one was safe; no one could be trusted. Neither friendship nor cooperation was possible. We lived like animals, or like Hobbes thought animals lived, and consequently our lives were, generally, 'solitary, poor, nasty, brutish, and short'.

And so, Hobbes claimed, we formed a contract, an agreement. The agreement, in all essentials, went like this: you agree to respect the life, liberty and property of other people on the condition that they in turn agree to respect your life, liberty and property. So, you agree not to kill other people and they agree not to kill you. You agree not to make other people into slaves and they agree not to make you into a slave. You agree not to steal other people's homes and possessions and they agree not to steal your home and possessions. Society is founded on a principle of 'You scratch my back and I'll scratch yours.' Or, at the very least, 'You refrain from sticking a knife in my back and I'll refrain from sticking one in yours.'

Hobbes was talking about a transformation from wildness – as he understood wildness to be – to civilization. The contract is what facilitates this transformation. If you accept the contract, then you accept certain limitations on your freedom. And the reason you do this is because your life becomes better as a result. That is the purpose and justification of society; that is the purpose and justification of morality.

Unfortunately, Hobbes's story about how we elevated ourselves above nature red and raw, and so became civilized instead of wild, has holes a fully grown 150-pound Brenin could have strolled comfortably through. Before the contract, so Hobbes's story goes, we were wild: we were nature red and raw, and our lives were solitary, poor, etc. After the contract, we were civilized and our lives were, consequently, much better.

One question that apparently never occurred to Hobbes was: how can those who are genuinely red in tooth and claw be brought to the negotiating table? And even more importantly: what would happen when you got them there? If, prior to the contract, we were all as nasty and brutish as Hobbes claimed, then wouldn't we use the sort of gathering necessary for making a contract as a golden opportunity to massacre a rival or two, or otherwise stamp our authority over the competition? The contractual situation would be a disaster, a bloodbath. Lives would become poorer and more solitary, nastier and more brutish, and, without a shadow of a doubt, shorter. That's the rub: contracts are only possible between civilized people. A contract, therefore, cannot be what made people civilized in the first place.

Despite the obvious truth that human civilization could never have been founded on a contract, some philosophers claim that it is useful to think of civilization as if it had been created in this way. The idea is that we can work out what a fair society – a just civilization – would look like by imagining that people had chosen to live by the rules of a contract, then working out what those rules would be. I used to think this way too, but not any more. The importance of the contract, I now think, lies in what it reveals about us – and, once again, this is a deeply unflattering facet of human nature.

Sometimes it is not what a theory says but what it shows that is important. Any theory will always be based on certain assumptions. Some of these may be explicit – the author of the theory may be aware of and acknowledge them. But there are always some assumptions that are not made explicit. Some assumptions may never be made explicit. The task of the philosopher is then, in essence, an archaeological one. Instead of digging into the soil, he digs deeper into the theory, uncovering, as far as his talent and persistence will allow, the hidden assumptions on which the theory has been based. This is what the theory shows, which is sometimes far more important than what it says.

What does the theory of the social contract show? It is supposed to be a story about the foundations and legitimacy of morality and civilization. The question is: what is it really about? The answer is: two things. One is more obvious than the other, but neither is flattering.

4

The first thing the theory of the social contract shows is our peculiarly human – or, more accurately, simian – obsession with power. The theory has a glaring consequence: you have no moral obligations to anyone significantly weaker than you. You contract with people for one of two reasons: because they can help you or because they can hurt you. You need some help? No worries: someone else will help you if you agree to help them when they need it. You want to safe-guard yourself against murder, attack and enslavement? No problem: others will agree not to do this to you if you agree not to do it to them. But this means that you have reason to contract only with people who can help you or hurt you. The whole idea of a contract makes sense only if we assume at least a rough equality of power between contractors. This is an idea on which just about everyone who believes in the contract agrees. The consequence is that anyone significantly weaker than you – anyone who can neither help nor hurt you – falls outside the scope of the contract.

But remember that the contract is supposed to provide the justification for civilization, society and morality. Those who fall outside the scope of the contract fall outside the scope of civilization. They lie outside the boundaries of morality. You have no moral obligations to those who are significantly weaker than you. That is the consequence of the contractual view of civilization. The purpose of morality is to garner more power: that is the first thing the theory of the social contract shows – the first assumption on which the theory is based. Wildness or civilization: which is really red in tooth and claw?

If we dig deeper, we find the second unacknowledged assumption. The contract is based on a deliberate sacrifice for an anticipated gain. You give up something only because you anticipate getting something better in return. You sell your freedom for protection, because for you protection is superior to freedom. To be afforded the protection of the contract, to have others protect your interests, you have to be willing to protect theirs. And this can cost you – time, energy, money, your safety, perhaps even your life. The sacrifices you make to be afforded the protection of the contract are not always minimal; sometimes they are significant. You make them only because you believe you will get more in return.

But here is the critical loophole. You don't really have to sell your freedom. You don't really have to make these sacrifices. What is crucial is not that you make your sacrifices, but that other people believe that you do. I'll watch your back, you say, if you'll watch mine. But it doesn't matter whether you really watch their back. What matters is that they believe you are watching it. The truth of your sacrifice is irrelevant. In the contract, image is everything. If you can acquire the rewards of the contract without making the requisite sacrifices, then you will, clearly, be at an advantage over the poor schmuck who actually does sacrifice their time, energy, money and safety. The contract – by its very nature – rewards deception. This is a deep, structural feature of the contract. If you can deceive, you garner the benefits of the contract while accruing none of the costs.

Cheaters never prosper, we tell ourselves. But the ape in us knows it's not true. Clumsy, untutored, cheats never prosper. They are discovered and suffer the consequences. They are ostracized, excluded, despised. But what we apes despise is the clumsiness of their efforts, the ineptness, the gaucherie. The ape in us does not despise the cheating itself; on the contrary, it admires it. The contract does not reward deception; it rewards skilful deception.

The contract is supposedly what makes us civilized human beings. But the contract also supplies an unvarying pressure towards deception. That which made us civilized turned us also into deceivers. But, at the same time, the contract can work only if deception is the exception rather than the rule. If everyone was always successfully deceiving everybody else, any possibility of social order or cohesion would break down. So the contract turned us also into detectors of deception. The drive to become ever more skilful deceivers is accompanied by the ability to become ever more skilful detectors of deception. Human civilization, and ultimately human intelligence, are the products of an arms race – and the primary warheads are lies. If you are civilized and you are not a liar, then it is probably because you are not a good liar.

What does this say about us? What sort of animal would think of its most prized asset, morality, as grounded in a contract? What sort of animal would think that we can work out what a just or fair society would be like by thinking of it in terms of a hypothetical contract agreed to by its members? To a wolf, but apparently not an ape, the answer would be obvious: a deceiver.

5

I once wrote a book about the social contract. The inspiration was supplied by Brenin doing what he did best. On our first Christmas together in Ireland, we were travelling back to Wales to see my parents. Brenin always enjoyed going to Wales, despite some deep differences of opinion with Bonnie and Blue. My mother indulged him in ways I didn't; and it was here that he first discovered the wonders of cheese. Cheese, I found, was far and away his favourite thing to eat, easily eclipsing the beef I had been buying for him. When my mother would cook something that required cheese, Brenin's presence in the kitchen was non-negotiable. He would sit there, making a sound that is difficult to describe since no dog makes it. It was a short, sharp sequence of something midway between a bark and a howl. Wolves don't bark – a bark is puppy behaviour and basically means, 'Come and back me up. There's something going on here that I'm really not too sure about.' Brenin didn't bark, though he did, every now and then, howl. But when he got excited – and cheese would set him off every time – he would emit a staccato series of 'Whoa, whoa, whoa, whoa, whoa . . .' This would be accompanied by the occasional bounce, and by something I had never seen him do before, and never imagined that he ever would: he sat up and begged. Eventually, my mother would toss him a piece of cheese and the whole process would begin again. This would entertain him for hours, if the meal took long enough to prepare. Eventually, meal preparation became tangential to the issue. Her presence in the vicinity of the refrigerator was enough to set him off.

This Christmas, we were travelling by Irish Ferries, from Rosslare to Pembroke. The ferry trip generally took around four hours. I had left Brenin in the car, since it was either that or the cages on the car deck – he wasn't allowed upstairs with me. This was something I had done several times before, with no adverse consequences. I would generally take him for a long walk on the beach at Rosslare before we boarded, to tire him out a bit. On this occasion, however, about ten minutes or so before we docked in Pembroke, as we were heading up the Milford Haven waterway, I looked up from my book and there was Brenin, trotting happily through the upper passenger lounge, in the general direction of the restaurant. Several employees of Irish Ferries trailed in his wake, pretending they were trying to catch him, but in reality keeping a safe distance. I called out his name and, as with the notorious Hungry Man incident of five years earlier, he froze in mid-stride and looked over towards me with, slowly dawning on his face, the Wile E. comprehension that he was busted.

I had left the window of the car open just a little to give Brenin some air. At some point during the crossing, he had forced the window down, and climbed out. The car deck was supposedly locked, but I figured they must have opened it as we were travelling up the waterway, which allowed Brenin to escape. There he managed to navigate his way up four flights of stairs to the upper passenger lounge, perhaps looking for me, or, more likely, following the smell of food. I dread to think what might have happened had he actually made it to the restaurant. I remembered all too well what could happen in classes if a student was carrying food in a backpack they had neglected to fasten securely. I could picture diners running screaming from the ferry restaurant, with Brenin, paws on table, cheerfully devouring their abandoned food, beginning with the cheese-based dishes, of course.

On the way back after Christmas, I decided to forestall any possibility of carnage at the restaurant by making sure that the windows of the car were, this time, open only a fraction. As it turned out, this was a serious error of judgement on my part. Brenin tore the car apart, quite literally. By the time he had finished, and I had been alerted to what was happening, there was nothing left inside that was recognizably a car. The seats were torn to pieces, the seat belts were all chewed through and he had ripped down the padding on the ceiling with the result that it was almost impossible to see out. In addition, he had slashed open a big bag of dog food and spread its contents into every nook and cranny.

I was called down to the car deck by the desperately amused ferry employees, and stared incredulously at the inside of my car – or what remained of it – for a few minutes. I noticed that the attendant on the car deck was carrying a knife and I asked him if I could borrow it. I needed to cut down the dangling shreds of the ceiling if I was going to have any hope of seeing out on the attempted drive back home. The attendant seemed strangely reluctant to part with his knife and on examination it turned out that he thought I was going to kill Brenin. As if! I explained – apparently shock causes me to switch to lecturer mode – that while I wasn't particularly enthralled with the way events had transpired, it was not something for which I could hold Brenin responsible. Brenin was not the sort of creature who could be morally responsible, I told the smirking car-deck guy. He was what's known as a moral patient, but not a moral agent. Brenin didn't understand what he was doing and so didn't understand that it was wrong. He just wanted out. Brenin, like other animals, is the sort of creature that has rights – a right to a certain kind of treatment and lifestyle – but he does not have concomitant responsibilities. Then I did the only thing a self-respecting philosopher could do in these circumstances: I went home and wrote a book about it.

The basic idea was finding a way to get animals included in the social contract by making the contract fairer. Imagine there is a group of you and you have just ordered a pizza. How do you make sure everyone gets a fair slice? Here's an easy way. Let one person slice it, but also make sure that he or she gets their slice last. If they don't know which slice they are going to get, then they can't arrange things in their favour. They have no option but to slice the pizza fairly. Now imagine the pizza is society. How do you ensure that the society you live in is a fair one? Just as we ensured a fair slicing of the pizza by making sure that the person who sliced it didn't know which slice they were going to get, so we could ensure a fair society by allowing a person to choose how it is to be organized, but by making sure that when they choose this they don't know who they are going to be in this society. This imaginative device was originally developed by the Harvard philosopher the late John Rawls. He called it the 'original position'.

Rawls uses the original position as a way of making the

contract fairer: for Rawls, social justice reduces to fairness. My argument was that Rawls had overlooked a source of unfairness in his development of the original position. Rawls insists on excluding knowledge of who you are and what you value when you choose how society is to be organized. You don't know if you are going to be male or female, black or white, rich or poor, intelligent or stupid, and so on. Nor do you know f you are a religious person or an atheist, selfish or altruistic, etc. But he still allows that you know what you are and what you can do – you know you are human and you know you are rational. My argument was, in effect, that if you wanted to make the contract truly fair you had to exclude this latter sort of knowledge also. Moreover, I argued that Rawls was implicitly committed to excluding this sort of know-ledge, even though he thought he wasn't. So the upshot was the development of a form of Rawlsian contractarianism that Rawls would have hated. The benefits, however, involved not just including animals in the contract but also the sorts of humans that traditional versions of the contract excluded: infants, the senile, the insane, etc. In short: the weak.

6

The resulting book was *Animal Rights: A Philosophical Defence*. If you can find a first edition, you'll see Brenin on the cover. Though not my first book, it was the one that really got my career back on track after my seven-year party in Alabama. And the only price I had to pay was a worthless car and a lifetime without meat.

That was the real sting in the tail of Brenin's appetite for destruction that day. Of course, the lesson wouldn't have sunk in unless I was already thinking about social-contract views of morality – in fact I was teaching a graduate course on them at the time. But this unfortunate confluence of events entailed a rather bleak future as a vegetarian. If I was in the original position – my newer, fairer version of the original position – I wouldn't choose a world in which animals are bred and raised for meat. They live miserable lives and die horrible deaths. And, since knowledge of species has to be excluded behind the veil of ignorance, for all I know in the original position I could be one of those animals. If you are in the original position it would be irrational to choose such a world. Therefore such a world is immoral. This was rather unfortunate, from my point of view, since I miss juicy steaks and fried chicken. But morality sometimes has a tendency to be inconvenient.

I was even a vegan for a while and, morally speaking, I really should still be one: it's the only consistent moral position on animals. But while I'm not as bad a person as I might be, I'm really not as good a person as I should be. I did try to exact revenge on Brenin by making him become a vegetarian too; but he wasn't having any of it. He refused, point blank, to eat the vegetarian dog meal I presented to him if it was on its own – and who can blame him? If I had mixed it up with a can of Pedigree Chum things would have been different, but that, of course, would have defeated the object of the exercise. In the end, we compromised: I became a vegetarian; he became a piscetarian. I would mix up vegetarian dry meal with a can of tuna – dolphin-friendly, obviously, and not yellowfin because of the mercury levels – and, sometimes, a few lumps of cheese. I hope he didn't miss meat as much as I did – and, in fact, still do. I suspect he actually preferred his new diet – especially on those days I added in the cheese. If not, well, perhaps he should have thought about that when he was eating my car – and to hell with whatever I said to the car-deck guy.

Was it immoral of me to impose a diet on him? Some have told me it was. But consider the alternative. A couple of cups of meat-based dog meal plus a can of meat a day must have added up to several cows during the course of the rest of his life – even allowing for the fact that dry dog meal probably doesn't contain anything like the amount of meat it claims. Brenin seemed to enjoy his new food, devouring it in much the same way as before, and I'm pretty sure a can of tuna tastes far better than a can of dog meat anyway. So, the new diet could be adopted at minimal, if any, inconvenience to him and didn't require the death of several cows. If Brenin had refused to eat, or eaten less, or lost weight or become sick, then that would have been a very different matter. But, in short, the choice was between balancing some relatively trivial interests of Brenin against a vital interest of the cows. And that, in essence, is the moral case for vegetarianism: the vital interests animals have in avoiding miserable lives and horrible deaths outweighs the relatively trivial interests humans have in the pleasures of their palate. Of course, given that he was a piscetarian rather than a vegetarian, the new regime was a little harsh on the tuna. But they have much better lives than cows – or, at least, so I told myself.

7

The contract, I tried to show earlier, is really about two things: power and deception. My book, like pretty much everything else written about the contract in recent years, is about how to minimize the impact of disparities of power on moral decision-making. But this leaves the real problem untouched. You can't address what is really wrong with the contract simply by trying to make it fairer. The real problem is deception and what underlies it: calculation. The contract, I now think, is a device invented by apes to regulate the interactions between apes.

Thinking about what is right and wrong through the prism of the contract gives us, in essence, a vision of morality as designed for strangers – the purpose of morality is to regulate the interactions between people who barely know each other and don't particularly like each other. And if we think of morality in this way, of course we are going to arrive at the idea that justice – fairness – is the primary moral virtue: the 'first virtue', as Rawls put it, of social institutions. Morally speaking, how should strangers act to each other except with fairness?

However, in addition to a morality for strangers there is also a morality for those of the pack. Hobbes thought of nature as red in tooth and claw. When I think of nature, I think of six-week-old Brenin, the day I brought him back to my house for the first time: like a big, brown, cuddly, destructive teddy bear. For that is how he was prior to our mutual accommodation; before he was brought into my civilization. Nature is no more red and raw than what we call civilization; and there is no war of each against all. The lives of wolves can be short, but so too can ours. They are not solitary and are poor only in the way we measure things.

By the time Brenin and I had spent an hour or so together in the house on that May afternoon, I already loved the cuddly little nemesis of curtains and air-conditioning systems. I always would. He was not, of course, in any position to help me, and he could hurt me – as he already had – only in the pocket; and there was nothing I could do to change that. If there ever was a contract between us, then it was peripheral, and based on a morality that was more basic and more visceral. This morality preached not justice but loyalty.

When I made Brenin become a piscetarian, the decision was unusual in this respect. It was one of the few occasions on which I would put the interests of animals that I had never met and would never meet over and above the interests of my wolf. In this instance, I placed justice over loyalty. Admittedly I did so only because I decided that the demands of loyalty in this case were so attenuated – Brenin could adopt this new diet at little, if any, inconvenience to him – and the demands of justice were so unequivocal. But this, as I said, was rare. As I like to tell my students when we discuss moral dilemmas, if you had ever found yourself in a lifeboat situation with me and Brenin, you would have been s**t out of luck. They think I'm joking.

One of the hardest tasks in morality is to balance the demands of strangers with the demands of the pack: the requirements of justice with the insistent tug of loyalty. It is clear that philosophy, throughout much of its history, has emphasized that morality is for strangers. This, I think, is no accident but stems from our simian pedigree. When you think of society as a collection of strangers, then you will think of morality as a form of calculation whereby we try and work out what is the best outcome – by some standard of 'best' – for all concerned. And calculation is what the ape in us does best. We don't look at our fellow apes; we watch them. We scheme, we conspire, we compute probabilities, we gauge possibilities; and all the while we wait for an opportunity to take advantage. The most important relationships in our lives are gauged in terms of surplus and deficit, profit and loss. What have you done for me lately? Do you fulfil me? What do I gain from being with you, and what do I lose? Can I do better? Calculation directed at society as a whole – moral rather than prudential calculation – is simply an extension of this basic skill. For us apes, it is natural to think in contractual terms, because the contract is nothing but a deliberate sacrifice for an anticipated gain. The idea of the contract is just a codification – a making explicit – of something that lies deep within us. Calculation runs to the core of the contract and to the heart of the ape in us. The contract is an invention by apes for apes – it can say nothing at all about the relationship between an ape and a wolf.

Why do we, at least some of us, love our dogs? Why did I love Brenin? I would like to think – and here I must lapse again into metaphor – that our dogs call out to something in the deepest recesses of a long-forgotten part of our soul. Here there dwells an older us – a part of us that was there before we became apes. This is the wolf that we once were. This wolf understands that happiness cannot be found in calculation. It understands that no truly significant relationship can ever be based on a contract. First there is loyalty. And this we must respect though the heavens fall. Calculation and contracts always come afterwards – as the simian part of our soul follows on from the lupine.

6

The Pursuit of Happiness and Rabbits

1

During the years in Ireland, Brenin was in his prime. He had grown truly massive, standing thirty-five inches at the shoulder and weighing close on 150 pounds. He was as tall as the Great Danes with which I'd grown up, but he was much more powerfully built. His legs were long, like his mother's, and on the end of them were feet the size of my fists; but he had thickened out and taken the bulk of his father. His head was a broad wedge and found itself perched on massive shoulders. His chest was deep and his hips were slim. He reminded me, more than anything, of a bull. In fact, when I thought of how he had changed from his youthful Alabama days to now, it always brought to mind Dylan Thomas's poem 'Lament' and its account of the transformation of the man from spring-tailed tom to hillocky bull. The youthful strip of black that ran down his snout had faded, but was still discernible, and framing it were the same strange, almond eyes. I don't have many photographs of Brenin – I didn't do photos in those days – but when I think back and try to fix his image firmly in mind, what I get are triangles. Bobbing around at the forefront of my consciousness are always triangles: the triangle of his head and snout; the triangles of his ears above, the triangle of his lateral torso, sloping down from his shoulders to his tail; the triangle of his frontal torso, sloping down to his legs and huge feet. And the black line of his snout and his yellow almond eyes were the focal point around which all these triangles were organized.

After we had been in Cork for about a year, I decided Brenin needed a friend; one with more legs and a colder nose than I. Sifting through the *Cork Examiner* – just as five years before I had sifted through the *Tuscaloosa News* – I saw an advert for 'Malamutes'. This was both surprising and disturbing. A malamute is an Arctic dog, a sled dog similar to a husky, but much taller and more massive. More importantly, 'malamute' was still Brenin's official cover story – that's what I told anyone who asked what he was. The Irish, for some reason, are terrified of large dogs. If anyone had found out that Brenin was a wolf, we'd probably have been run out of the country, or worse. There was a corner shop I used to pop into with Brenin on my daily walk into work. One day the board outside was emblazoned with the headline 'Wolf'. This was an ultimately very sad story of a (rather small) wolf hybrid that had escaped from its home and gone walkabout around the countryside of Northern Ireland. Though this was in the North, the Republic's media was in a frenzy, and so too was the woman who served me my daily can of Coke and a cheese sandwich. It was the usual uninformed claptrap, uttered without blinking at Brenin, to whom she had become quite accustomed. What about the children? They should be banned. They're killers. In the end, the wolf was shot by some idiot farmer to whom it had strolled up, perhaps to ask if he had any food. And the shopkeepers and children of Erin could sleep soundly in their beds once more. So, much like Clark Kent, Brenin had very good reasons to want his identity kept secret. 'Malamute' was my way of doing that. Malamutes were virtually unknown in Ireland, and I was counting on things staying that way.

The next day saw us driving up to a small village just outside Ennis in County Clare – about three hours away. The father of the litter did indeed turn out to be a malamute: a big brown one, almost as big as Brenin, in fact. Inevitably, Brenin hated him. The mother, on the other hand, was no malamute at all, but a small German shepherd; perhaps the ugliest shepherd I've ever seen.

In my experience, when you have two mismatched parents, the pups always grow up looking like the worst one. So I wasn't going to touch them. However, when I saw the puppies, I changed my mind. They were housed in a garage and covered in filth and fleas. I decided I had to rescue one and picked the biggest female from the litter. I'm a sucker for puppies. Nevertheless, I drove home with a distinctly sinking feeling in my stomach. Great, I thought, I'm stuck with an ugly German shepherd for the next decade or so. But, in fact, my luck was in that week. She grew up to be the nicest, bravest, most intelligent dog you could ever meet – and, for that matter, not at all ugly. I named her Nina, short for Karenina, after Karenin, the dog in *The Unbearable Lightness of Being*, one of my favourite books, who was in turn named after Anna Karenina.

The Pursuit of Happiness and Rabbits

I had wanted to acquire another dog primarily so Brenin would have some canine company. But, initially, he was less than appreciative. When she was a puppy, Nina tormented him constantly, never giving him a moment's peace. In no time at all, she had learned to use his wild heritage against him, discovering how to make him regurgitate his food. A few seconds of frantic licking of his muzzle – Brenin would try to avert his head, but Nina was relentless – and up would come his dinner, which Nina then gobbled up with delight: a scene that managed to be simultaneously poignant and revolting. Nina quickly became a very fat puppy and Brenin a very thin wolf. Eventually Brenin found a part of the garden that Nina couldn't access, since it required him to leap up a four-foot nearly vertical bank. He used to retreat there for hours on end – especially after dinner – with Nina jumping and yipping in a futile manner at the bottom. This respite lasted only a few weeks – Nina eventually growing big enough to claw her way up to join him. But it did allow Brenin time to put back on the weight he had lost.

Despite the unremitting torment, however, Brenin was very protective towards Nina, allowing neither other dogs nor other people to come anywhere near her. And this brings me to my second slice of luck that week. One night, around midnight, a few days after the arrival of Nina, there was a noise in our back garden. The garden was surrounded on all sides by a large hedge – eight feet or more tall – and it was impossible to enter it by accident. I didn't hear the noise, but Brenin did, shooting to his feet and jumping up at the window, front feet perched on the sill. When I let him out, he ran over to the bank at the end of the garden, the place where he used to lie to escape Nina, disappeared behind a tree and reappeared dragging a man, whom he then pinned to the ground. I hesitate to relate the next part, since I really don't come out of it very well. In my defence, I'd lived in the US so long that I was still in an American mindset. My first thought was, 'Oh, my God, what if he has a gun? He's going to shoot my boy!' So I ran into the garden and started kicking him, screaming Americanisms like, 'Don't move, mother-fucker!' But, of course, he did move: it would be difficult not to when you have a wolf at your throat and a madman kick-ing you while screaming obscenities. Eventually, the whole thing calmed down. I got the guy – a big man, around my age, who might conceivably have given me some trouble if I had been on my own – in a full nelson: one arm behind his back, the other bent over his shoulder. 'What are you doing in my garden?' I asked. 'Nut-tin,' he said. So I marched him out of the house and threw him into the street.

I had no telephone at the time, so couldn't have called the police. But as soon as the adrenalin rush had died down, I started to realize why that would have been a bad idea anyway. The enormity of what I had just done started to sink in. If we had still been in America and we had tackled an intruder in this way, we would almost certainly have been congratulated by neighbours and police alike. But I didn't think it was going to wash in Ireland, where they tend to take a much dimmer view of using a wolf to savage interlop-ers. Luckily, this was a cold night in late October and the guy was wearing a big coat. I don't think Brenin had been able to do much damage through it – at least, I didn't see any obvi-ous blood when I threw him out. Still, I thought, all things considered, this might not be a bad time to get Brenin the hell out of Dodge. Possibly, this was an overreaction, but the inci-dent with the wolf hybrid in the North had left me more than a little paranoid. So I planned to leave him with my parents for a few weeks, until things had died down a little. I hurriedly packed a bag and prepared for an overnight drive to the ferry at Rosslare, with Brenin and Nina, where I thought we would catch the 9 a.m. sailing and be safely out of the country before the Guards – the Garda Siochana, the Irish police – knew where we were.

Then there was a knock on the door. The Guards were here already. I pulled back the curtains and peered around to the front door, my mind racing with thoughts such as just how, exactly, does one conduct oneself in a siege situation? And, indeed, how exactly does one engineer a siege situation when one doesn't have a gun? Or, for that matter, a hostage? However, I needn't have worried. It was the woman who lived next door. It emerged that the man Brenin and I had assaulted was her estranged husband. She told me that he would show up every now and then – usually after he'd had a skinful – to beat her up. Even better, at least from the perspective of my wolf and me, was that there was a restraining order in effect and he wasn't supposed to be within 100 feet of her house – not that this, apparently, had done much good. So, I figured, the chances of him calling the Guards were pretty low, and I decided to put our midnight exodus to Rosslare on hold.

Even now, I can't believe how lucky I was that night. Admittedly, anyone in my garden at midnight wasn't going to be up to much good. But even so, would you really want us as neighbours? What if it had been a child in your garden? That is what the shopkeeper would have said. I'm inclined to think everything would have been fine. Brenin didn't get to meet that many children in his life, but the ones he did meet he always treated with a gentleness and consideration that impressed me. Certainly, after this night, he got to know the little boy next door quite well – and both the boy and his mother became very fond of Brenin.

Nonetheless, the episode did make me aware of something that, in hindsight, had probably been sloshing around in my preconscious mind for some time. Brenin and I were just a little too volatile. And because of this, we were just a little too dangerous. If we were cowboys, people would have described us as having itchy trigger fingers. That's what pops into my mind when I think of my actions on that night. I was just a little too quick to jump in, my flying feet just a little too eager to support Brenin's flashing teeth. Our sense of loyalty to each other now far outstripped our sense of justice to others. We had become a pack; a nation of two. And those outside our nation didn't matter to us as much as they should have mattered.

After this incident, many of you might say that Brenin had no place in a civilized society. You might be right, but if so I would add the caveat – neither did I. That night marked the beginning of our gradual withdrawal from the world of humans. This world – and I have to be honest about this – had begun to disgust me. It disgusted me that there was, in effect, a shoot-to-kill policy on Brenin. It disgusted me that I had to be a running man – constantly ready to pack my bags and take flight. These thoughts were, of course, melodramatic overreactions. In reality, they were excuses that allowed me to do something I wanted to do anyway. The real change was not in the world but in me. From the gregarious party animal of my Alabama days, I had become something quite different: a loner, a misfit, a misanthrope. I was someone who didn't belong. I was sick of humans. I needed to get their stench out of my nostrils.

We moved out of Cork City a few months later. The woman

next door and her son were very sorry to see us go. When your life is made miserable by a big and vicious dog, and your civilization won't do anything about it, then sometimes what you need is a bigger and more vicious dog to watch your back.

2

I bought a small house, a gate lodge on the Knockduff peninsula, a few miles from a town called Kinsale on the south coast of Ireland, and about twenty miles from Cork City. I would like to say that I fell in love with the place as soon as I saw it. The truth was that I had been looking for a place for some time and things always kept falling through at the last minute, largely due to the vacillation of the vendors. So, when I saw the house in Kinsale – and after having looked at it for less than two minutes – my actual reaction was: it'll do. I made an offer and had it accepted within ten minutes. The house was a gate lodge built in the 1700s, with three-foot-thick stone walls, rendered white, with exposed stone around the doors and windows. It had brown stable doors at front and back and, because of the thickness of the walls, the window sills were three feet deep. At the slightest disturbance outside, Brenin and Nina used to stand up at the stable doors, big paws hanging out over the edge. Or, if the doors were closed, they would jump up on to the sills and stare menacingly out. They were almost certainly the best burglar deterrents in the world. In fact, they deterred pretty much everyone. Understandably enough, Colm, the postman, was a little reluctant to get out of his van, so he would sit there and beep his horn until I waved him the all clear. Eventually, I put up a mailbox where he could deposit the post without stepping outside his mobile sanctuary.

The essence of the house was easily captured in two words: tiny and basic. I think even Brenin and Nina found it a tad primitive. There were only five rooms in total: living room, bathroom, two bedrooms and a kitchen, each of which was very small. By some quirk, whether of history or bizarre intent, the bathroom was the biggest room in the house. There was a central-heating system that worked when it felt like it; and when it didn't I would have to go outside to the boiler and negotiate with the family of rats that had made its home in the boiler room for permission to fix the problem (Brenin and Nina quickly sorted out that particular difficulty for me). This was the first house I had owned. People thought I was mad: the price I paid for this tiny, damp and draughty house was considered extortionate, even for the fashionable district of Kinsale, 'The Gourmet Capital of Ireland', where, unaccountably, literally scores of upmarket restaurants had decided to make their home. But I needn't have worried. With the Irish property market the way it was in those days, I could have bought a chicken coop and still made bucket-loads of money.

It was the location I really loved. The lodge was a couple of miles or so outside Kinsale on the Rathmore peninsula. The main house to which the lodge was attached was derelict. This meant that Brenin, Nina and I had a couple of hundred acres of rolling countryside to run in every day. We just had to walk out of the door to find ourselves in the middle of barley fields as far as the eye could see. These would slope down to woodland and beyond that was the sea. Brenin and Nina quickly discovered that where there's barley, there are always rats. And they also quickly worked out that to see rats in the barley, you need a synoptic view. And to get this, they needed to bounce. The movement scared the rats and made them scurry, and from their momentarily elevated vantage points, Brenin and Nina were able to see the movement in the barley and pounce accordingly. All I could see of them was the occasional leap into the air, quickly followed by their submergence, like salmon leaping out of a sea of barley. I think it is impossible to be around that much joy without being lifted by it – although the rats might have felt differently.

The barley fields sloped down to the wood. On the edge of the wood was a rabbit warren. Here the behaviour of Brenin and Nina changed accordingly. From the bouncing of the barley fields, they went into stalking mode – trying to sneak up on any careless rabbit sunning itself on the open ground. Brenin was a lot more adept at this than Nina, who would usually give the game away by charging much too early. And for this I was very grateful. Since writing the *Animal Rights* book, I was now officially, and publicly, against the killing of animals for sport or food – even rats, although I tended to turn a blind eye to that when they were housed in my boiler room. Apparently, I was far more equivocal on the issue of violence towards wife-beating midnight intruders. But I was, nonetheless, strongly against cruelty to animals. Incredibly, I had become even weirder than I was before – a moral vegetarian, the strangest of the strange, condemned to live out the rest of my miserable existence without the gustatory pleasures of animal flesh. And, as I kept reminding Brenin, after I had scuppered some or other of his rabbit-catching stratagems, it was entirely his fault.

3

When I left Alabama for Ireland, the plan had been to find a house in the country, as far away from civilization as possible, and where there was absolutely, positively nothing to do except write. And, for the most part, I stuck to that plan pretty well. There were girlfriends, but they came into my life and left it again with a regularity by which you could set your watch and an inevitability on which you could bet your bottom dollar. They came into my life presumably because I was urbane and witty – at least when I could be bothered – and still unusually handsome, at least for a professional academic, with a face not yet ruined by years of alcohol. They left it because they quickly realized I felt little for them and saw little in them other than a convenient sexual release. I was in no fit state to share my life with humans. I had other concerns.

The truth is, I suppose, that I've always been a natural misanthrope. This is not something of which I'm proud, and not an aspect of my character that I seek, or have sought, to cultivate. But it's there and it's unmistakable. With a small number of exceptions, my relationships with other people have always been permeated by the sense – a vague, brooding comprehension – that what I am doing is killing time. This is how alcohol first insinuated its way into my life. I always had to get drunk to spend any time at all with friends, whether in Wales, Manchester, Oxford or Alabama. This is not to say I didn't enjoy myself – on the contrary, I had a blast. But I'm pretty sure it would have been different without the alcohol. And this isn't just some stuck-up academic talking, only wanting to associate with those he regards as his intellectual peers. Academics bore me even more. The fault is not with any of the people I have called my friends. It is with me. There is something lacking in me. And, over the years since, it has slowly dawned on me that the choices I have made, and the life I have lived, have been a response to this lack. What is most significant about me, I think, is what I am missing.

My choice of career is almost certainly an expression of this lack. With the possible exception of the higher reaches of pure mathematics or theoretical physics, one can scarcely imagine anything more inhuman than philosophy. Its worship of logic in all its cold, crystalline purity; its determination to stride the bleak and icy mountaintops of theory and abstraction: to be a philosopher is to be existentially deracinated. When I think of a philosopher, I think of Bertrand Russell, sitting down all day every day for five years at the British Library, writing *Principia Mathematica*, an unbelievably difficult and ingenious attempt – probably unsuccessful – to derive mathematics from set theory. It took Russell eighty-six pages to prove, using only the apparatus of set theory, what he, sarcastically, called the 'occasionally useful' proposition that one plus one equals two. So you can imagine how long the book is. Or I think of Nietzsche, an itinerant cripple wandering from one country to another, without friends, without family, without money; his work, after a promising start, garnering only rejection and derision. And imagine what it cost them. Intellectually, Russell was never the same again. And Nietzsche descended into madness – although, admittedly, syphilis may have played a role here. Philosophy is withering. Philosophers should be offered condolences rather than encouragement.

So I suspect there was always a natural misanthrope

within just waiting for his chance. He was kept pretty much in his box during my early years. But when I got to Ireland, his time had come. Given that I was useless at mathematics – a year studying engineering at Manchester had conclusively demonstrated this – philosophy was probably the only career that allowed me to suitably foster this aspiring misanthrope. My self-imposed exile from the world of humans was simply a logical extension of this. And Brenin – the big, bad wolf – became a symbolic expression of this exile. Brenin was not just my best, and only, friend. I was beginning to understand myself in terms of what he represented: the rejection of a human world of warmth and friendship, and the embrace of a world of ice and abstraction. I had become a man of the Arctic. My little house in the country – my draughty, glacial house – with a heating system that rarely worked, and didn't heat the house even when it did, was a suitable physical shell for my new emotional detachment.

My parents, bless them, were terribly worried about me. The constant refrain on my increasingly infrequent visits home was: how can you possibly be happy living like that?

4

According to many philosophers, happiness is intrinsically valuable. What they mean is that happiness is valuable for its own sake, not for the sake of anything else. Most of the things we value, we do so because of other things they can do for us or get for us. We value money, for example, only because of other things we can purchase with it: food, shelter, security, perhaps, some of us think, even happiness. We value medicine not in itself but because of the role it can play in promoting a return to health. Money and medicine are instrumentally valuable, but they are not intrinsically valuable. Some philosophers think that only happiness is intrinsically valuable: happiness is the only thing that we value for itself and not for the sake of anything else that it might allow us to get.

Since those days of the late 1990s, when my parents worried about me, happiness has acquired a much higher profile, not so much in philosophy but in the wider culture. It's even become big business. Millions of acres of forest have been sacrificed on its altar, bringing us all those books that tell us how we can pull off the happiness trick. Some governments have got in on the act, sponsoring studies that tell us that despite the fact that we are, materially, so much richer than our forebears, we are no happier than they were: proof that money can't buy you happiness is a very useful thing for any government to have.

Finally, and inevitably, academics, who know a gravy train when they smell one, have jumped on board: accosting – or, more accurately, getting their postgraduate students to accost – people on the street and asking them impertinent questions like, 'When are you happiest?' Coyness and discretion are, of course, not highly ranked in the pantheon of early twenty-first-century Western virtues, and many people actually respond to this question. Apparently – and this is something on which all studies concur – they're happiest when they're having sex and unhappiest when talking to their boss. And if they're having sex with their boss while talking to him or her, it is not clear what they are: bittersweet opportunists, possibly.

What must we think happiness is, if we answer, 'When I'm

having sex,' to the question, 'When are you happiest?'? We must be thinking of happiness as a feeling; specifically, the feeling of pleasure – for this is what sex produces if you're doing it remotely well. Similarly, the unhappiness involved in talking to your boss presumably has something to do with the feelings of unease and worry, or perhaps nausea and contempt, this conversation involves. Happiness and unhappiness reduce to feelings of a certain sort. Suppose that we combine this idea with the philosophers' claim that happiness is intrinsically valuable – probably the one thing in life we want for its own sake and not for the sake of anything else. Then we arrive at a simple conclusion: the most important thing in life is to feel a certain way. The quality of your life, whether your life is going well or badly, is a matter of what feelings you have.

One useful way of characterizing humans is as a particular type of addict or junkie. This, with the possible exception of some of the great apes, is true of no other animal. Humans are not, in general, pharmacological junkies – although, obviously, some are. But they are happiness junkies. Happiness junkies share with their ordinary, pharmacological cousins an insistent craving for something that really doesn't do them that much good and isn't really all that important anyway. But, in one clear sense, happiness junkies are worse. A pharmacological junkie has a mistaken conception of where his or her happiness comes from. Happiness junkies have a mistaken conception of what happiness is. Both are united by a failure to appreciate what is most important in life.

Happiness junkies come in all shapes and sizes, and from all walks of life. There are no tracks on arms, legs or feet to identify happiness junkies. They don't need to shoot up or snort. Some humans are 18–30 happiness junkies. They head out every Friday and Saturday nights to the city centre of wherever they live and get drunk and/or high, have sex, or, if that doesn't work out (and maybe even if it does), get into a fight. Then, once or twice a year, they'll travel to Ibiza, Corfu, Crete, Cancun or wherever they're supposed to go this year, and do exactly the same things, just with a little more intensity. This, for them, is what happiness is. Happiness is pleasure and pleasure is what it is all about.

You don't need to be 18–30 to be an 18–30 happiness junkie: anyone familiar with the demographics of Saturday night city centres or charter flights to Corfu can tell you that. Some humans stay 18–30 happiness junkies the whole of their lives. Others, however, as they become older, slower and weaker also become, as they see it, more sophisticated. First, they expand their conception of happiness beyond the nakedly hedonistic and decadent feelings that characterized the 18–30 years. For mature sophisticates, happiness doesn't consist only, or even primarily, in the feelings produced by sex, drugs and alcohol. Now they recognize more important feelings. The unambiguous yet often debilitating pleasures associated with drinking a small river of Stella become replaced by the more subtle frisson of pleasure induced by a glass or two of a good Latour. The stirring pleasures occasioned by having sex with people they barely know is replaced by the more refined pleasures of a relationship that is 'serious' and, indeed, in terms of its level of sexual activity, practically bordering on the sibling. The desire to 'burn, burn, burn like fabulous yellow roman candles exploding like spiders across the stars', as Kerouac once put it, is replaced by the sophisticated warm glow of watching their babies dribble, or mumble something that may or may not be their first word.

This growing sophistication is marked by an expansion in the kinds of feelings humans are willing to allocate to the category of happiness. But this is an expansion built on the original model. Whatever else happiness is, it is a feeling of some sort. This is what defines human beings: the perpetual and futile pursuit of feelings. No other animal does this. Only humans think feelings are so important.

One consequence of this obsessive focus on feelings is that humans have a tendency towards neurosis. This occurs when the focus shifts from the production of feelings to their examination. Are you genuinely happy with the way your life is going? Does your partner properly understand your needs? Do you really find fulfilment in raising your children? There is, of course, nothing wrong with examining your life. Life is all we have, and to live a good life is the most important thing of all. But characteristic of humans is a perverse interpretation of the form this examination must take: we think that examining our life is one and the same thing as examining our feelings. And when we examine our feelings, when we look inside and see what's there and what isn't there, the answer at which we arrive is often a negative one. We don't feel the way we want to, or the way we think we should. So what do we do? Good happiness junkies that we are, we go in search of the next fix: a toyboy or toygirl, a new motor, a new house, a new life – a new anything. For the junkie, happiness always comes with the new and exotic rather than the old and familiar. And if all else fails – and often it does – there is an army of highly remunerated professionals who are happy to tell us how we can get our next fix.

In short, perhaps the clearest and simplest characterization of the human species is this: humans are the animals that worship feelings.

5

Don't misunderstand me. I don't have anything against feelings, or sex. Neither, apparently, did Brenin. One evening in May, during the hottest two weeks I'd ever experienced in Ireland, Brenin disappeared. It was the only time he ever did this. I'd let him and Nina out of the garden, turned my back for a second, and he was gone. I saw his tail disappearing over the wall – a six-foot-high stone wall. I wasn't surprised he had managed to scale the wall. I was surprised he wanted to. He had never shown any inclination to escape before. By the time I ran on to the road, he was out of sight. So I put Nina in the Jeep and we drove around in search of him. We discovered him several miles down the road, *in flagrante delicto* with a white German shepherd. The owners were incensed – although, in my humble opinion, you really shouldn't expect anything good to come of leaving a bitch in season unattended in your garden.

It all worked out fine for the owners of the shepherd – they eventually made a fortune on the sale of the puppies. Brenin was, by now, famous in the Kinsale locality; and there was apparently no shortage of people who would pay an arm and a leg for one of his puppies. I, on the other hand, was saddled with another dog, because there was no way I wasn't going to take at least one of Brenin's progeny. I never had Brenin neutered because I didn't have the heart. That was predictably male of me. Men's eyes water at the very thought of neutering our dogs. But we are ready to send our bitches off for spaying at the drop of a hat – even though it's a far more serious and invasive procedure. And this is why, of course, I didn't have to worry about Brenin and Nina – I had poor old Nina spayed at soon as the vets told me it was safe to do so. I needed another dog like a hole in the head. As it was, Brenin and Nina could barely both fit in the back of the Jeep – even though I had taken the seats out. Any other dog would be sitting next to me in the front (and, you know, that's exactly what happened). And so, about three and a half months later, our pack acquired another member: Brenin's daughter. I named her Tess.

I was also saddled with a moral dilemma, which was more serious than the predicted inconvenience of another dog. I had not bred Brenin – despite various proposals from other wolf and wolf-hybrid owners – because I knew what his cubs were going to be like: him. I remembered very well what he had been like as a cub, and I knew most people wouldn't be in a position to spend the sort of time with his cubs that I had with him. As a result, I believed things would go very badly for his children. This is something that still haunts me today. I hope his children – they'll be old dogs now – are all right. I pray they have lived good lives. But I suspect not all of them have. And for this I am sorry.

Perhaps because he had little conception of the consequences, Brenin seemed to enjoy his sexual excursion. And he made repeated attempts to replicate the feat in the coming days. And then there was his crying himself to sleep when I wouldn't let him escape any more. So, who knows, if Brenin were able to take part in one of those happiness surveys, perhaps he would have answered, 'When I'm having sex,' to the question, 'When are you happiest?' If so, this would have been very unfortunate – he would have been truly happy only once. Of course, if he had grown up in the wild, the chances are he would have been even less happy: unless he was the pack's alpha male, he wouldn't have been allowed to have sex at all.

However, I suspect that what is in fact important for a wolf is not sex, or feelings of any sort. Unlike humans, wolves don't chase feelings. They chase rabbits.

6

People often asked me if Brenin was happy. What they actually meant, of course, was how could you take a wolf out of the wild – you cruel and irresponsible bastard – and force him to live an artificial life constrained by human culture and mores? I've already talked about this. But let's suppose that the objection is warranted. If it is, then we would expect that Brenin was at his happiest doing what comes naturally. Sex might be one of those things. But so too is hunting.

I spent a lot of time watching Brenin hunt, and tried to work out what, if anything, he must have been feeling when he did it. What did Brenin feel when he was stalking a rabbit? Rabbits are fast and slippery and can change direction on a sixpence. Flat out and in a straight line, Brenin was quicker, but even he didn't have the moves of your typical rabbit. So Brenin had to stalk. And the essence of stalking is to effect a certain kind of realignment of the situation in which you find yourself. Stalking is a matter of making the world one that is conducive to your strengths and indifferent to the strengths of your prey. This is an arduous process and, I suspect, one that is largely unpleasant rather than pleasant.

Brenin's patience was breathtaking. Most of the time he lay on the ground, his nose and front legs pointed towards the rabbit, muscles tensed and ready to spring. When the rabbit was otherwise distracted, he would inch closer and then lie motionless until there was another opportunity to move. It was not clear exactly how long this process would go on if uninterrupted, but I've watched him continue it for at least fifteen minutes. Brenin was trying to engineer a situation in which his strength – surprise and an astonishing acceleration over a short distance – were more important than the strength of the rabbit to change direction on a sixpence. Usually, and thankfully, the rabbit would get wind of him long before then. When he knew the game was up, Brenin would strike in an astonishing blur of postponed activity. Most of the time he would come away empty-handed.

If this is when Brenin was happy, then what was happiness for him? There was the agony of tension, the enforced rigidity of mind and body, the obligatory conflict between the intense desire to strike and the knowledge that this could bring disaster. What Brenin most wanted, he had to deny himself, over and over again. His agony would be alleviated only partially by his clandestine inching forward; and then, when he stopped, the process would begin all over again. If this is happiness, then it seems more agony than ecstasy.

Perhaps, someone might say, Brenin was only happy when he caught the rabbit. I hope not, because he did so only rarely. But his behaviour clearly indicated otherwise. Success or failure would always see him bounding up to me afterwards, in the same way, eyes blazing, jumping all over me in his excitement. That, I'm pretty sure, was a happy wolf – and, if so, his happiness had little to do with the delight of feeling his jaws close on the flesh of the rabbit.

Brenin's hunting reminded me more than anything of what I did in the other part of my life: philosophy. I stalked not rabbits but thoughts. Brenin stalked rabbits that were, often, too difficult for him to catch. I stalked thoughts that were too difficult for me to think. It is possible, if you put in enough effort, to force yourself to think things that you were unable to think before – unable to think precisely because they're too difficult for you. But it is a deeply unpleasant thing to do. It hurts. First, there is the prolonged unpleasantness that goes with thrashing around in an area that is just too demanding for you – the brackish and muddy waters of a swamp where you can find no landmarks and gain no purchase on the firm soil of shore. Then, perhaps after many weeks or months, the thought starts to come: it begins to be thought. Here is where the stalking commences. You feel the thought like an obstacle in your throat, slowly rising, rising; the sweet promise of release rising with it. But then you realize this is a dead end, and your blockage just sinks back down and sits inside you, hard, obdurate and unpleasant, like a bad meal. Then you see a new avenue and the hope rises again in you. You can feel the thought coming – almost, almost. But it is not yet ready and sinks back down inside you. You can't force a thought, any more than you can force a rabbit. A thought will come, and a rabbit will be caught, only when the time is right. But neither can you ignore the thought and simply wait for it; you have to keep up the pressure on it or it will never come. Eventually, if you are lucky and diligent, the thought will come, then you can think something that was too difficult for you to think before. The release is undeniable, but that was never what it was about. Soon you move on to the next thought and the unpleasantness begins all over again.

Happiness is not just pleasant; it is also deeply unpleasant. It is for me and I suspect it was for Brenin. By this, I don't mean the familiar piece of homespun wisdom about not being able to appreciate the good times unless you have also experienced the bad. Everyone knows that. The homespun wisdom claims a causal dependence between appreciation of the good and experience of the bad. Unless you have experienced unpleasant things, you will not be able to recognize good things when you encounter them. This is not what I mean by saying that happiness is unpleasant. Rather, I am claiming that happiness is itself partly unpleasant. This is a necessary truth about happiness: happiness couldn't be any other way. In happiness, pleasant and unpleasant aspects form an indissoluble whole. They cannot be separated without everything falling apart.

7

Brenin liked fighting. I suspect he was happy when he was fighting. This was too bad, because I never let him do it. I tried to excise this aspect of personality, but without any real success. And it was only when he became old and weak that I could really trust him around other large male dogs. But while this wasn't an aspect of his character that I, in any way, could commend, it was one that I did comprehend.

I was a pretty good amateur boxer when I was a kid and I used my skills as an occasional way of supplementing my income as a student – unlicensed bouts held in undisclosed movable locations in areas like Ancoats and Moss Side – though I tried to stay out of the latter; too many smart, fast black kids. You would put in fifty quid to enter and then fight several times during the night – at least, if you were lucky. If you win your first fight, you get your fifty back. If you win the second, you double it. A third fight will take you up to 200 – and that would keep me going for several months in those days. But as soon as you lose you're out. My goal was to try and win three fights. Then in the fourth fight I would cover up and run – take the loss and try to get out of there without too much damage before I ran into the good fighters later on in the evening.

The crowd, of course, didn't like it – and would register their displeasure, in the time-honoured way, with a chorus of boos, threats and questionings of my ancestry and sexuality. But what I remember most was not that, but the walk to the ring. The crowd would inevitably be baying for blood, and I would be so scared that my field of vision would close down into a narrow tunnel. My legs would feel awkward and hard to control. My breathing would be difficult and painful. And I would avoid vomiting only because I had already done so. These feelings and reactions would all persist through the preliminaries. But then, when I was standing in the corner of the ring, looking across at my opponent, just before the fight started and when any prospect of escape had vanished, there would be a wonderful feeling of calm that flowed through me, starting at my toes and fingers and washing all over me in waves.

It was a peculiar calm – for the fear never went away. It just didn't matter any more. When I fought, I was cocooned away inside a golden bubble of concentration. The fear was still there, but it was a calm and positive fear, and with it came a certain kind of exultation that is difficult to convey. The exultation stemmed from doing something that I did well, but at the same time knowing that I couldn't afford to drop off one whit from the limits of my ability. Perhaps the best way I have of describing this exultation is as a kind of knowing.

Fighting was never personal. Inside the golden bubble, you feel no animosity. It is an impersonal – intellectual – endeavour. To describe it as intellectual seems strange, but I do so because fighting embodies a certain kind of knowledge. This knowledge is peculiar to fighting. There is no other way of acquiring it. You know just how long the opponent holds out his hand after he has jabbed. You know this even though you can't see his hand. You know what he does with his feet when he throws his right cross – and you know this even though you are not looking at his feet. In your bubble of concentration, and at the limits of your physical and emotional abilities, you can know things you otherwise wouldn't know. He's held his hand out a fraction of a second too long after his jab and you slip your head outside and counter with a left cross inside his arm (those of you who understand what is going on will be able to work out from this description that I was a southpaw – at least if we assume the other guy was orthodox). If your punch connects with his jaw, a crisp, clean, connection, then you feel exultation. This is not because you hate your opponent: on the contrary, in your bubble of concentration, you feel nothing, neither for him nor against. You feel exultation because you are coldly, and calmly, terrified out of your wits. To fight is to know not just your opponent but your own existential predicament: it is to know that you are balanced on the edge of a precipice and that one false move in either direction will bring disaster.

When life is at its most visceral, and therefore also at its most vibrant, it is not possible to separate exultation from terror. The knowledge that ruin haunts your every move not only makes possible the most powerful forms of exultation; it fuses with – becomes part of – that exultation. Terror and exultation are two sides of the same coin; two aspects of the same *gestalt*. Exultation is never purely pleasant – it is necessarily also deeply unpleasant.

8

A theodicy is an attempt to find a reason for the unpleasantness of life. As the name suggests, theodicies traditionally appeal to God: He works in mysterious ways, is testing us, gave us free will and so on. But there also exist what we might think of as Godless theodicies – most famously, perhaps, that of Nietzsche, who saw pain and suffering as a necessary means to becoming stronger. All theodicies are, in the final analysis, acts of faith. They are because they all involve, explicitly or implicitly, the idea that life has a goal or purpose. Life has a meaning and the goal of a theodicy is to identify where – in that context – fear, pain and suffering are to be situated. One of the hardest things to do is not simply to learn that life has no meaning. It is to learn why the idea that it has – or should have – steers us away from what is truly important.

I am not trying to justify pain and suffering. I am not trying to provide a theodicy. Life has no meaning, at least not in the way people usually think of it, and so pain and suffering do not contribute to that meaning. Nonetheless, I was soon to learn that life can have value; and it can have value because of certain things that happen in it. Sitting in the long grass, watching Brenin stalking rabbits, taught me that it is important in life to make sure you chase rabbits and not feelings. What is best about our lives – the moments when we are, as we would put it, at our happiest – is both pleasant and deeply unpleasant. Happiness is not a feeling; it is a way of being. If we focus on the feelings, we will miss the point. But I was soon to learn a related lesson. Sometimes the most unpleasant moments of our lives are the most valuable. And they can be the most valuable only because they are the most unpleasant. There were many unpleasant moments to come.

7

A Season in Hell

1

By the time we had been there five years or so, our life in Ireland had settled into a routine that was both predictable and, from the point of view of my career, profitable. I would wake up in the morning when I felt like it. Then I would go for a run with Brenin and the girls, through the fields and down to the sea. After that I would drive into Cork and take care of whatever teaching commitments, if any, I had. Then I would go to the gym. I'd generally arrive home around 6 and then I would start writing. I'd carry on with this until around 2 a.m.

After Nina had come into the picture, I decided to leave Brenin at home when I went to work. His youthful destructiveness had declined considerably by now. Nina was admittedly doing her best to take up the slack, but even at her worst, her destructive ingenuity and power never really compared to Brenin's. He wasn't happy about being left at home, and I did miss his presence in my office and the classroom. Sometimes, in the middle of a lecture, I would look over to the corner of the room, expecting to see him, and suffer a momentary jolt of shock until I remembered he was at home. But I thought it would be very unfair on a young dog like Nina to be left all on her own in the house – especially when she could see Brenin and me driving off in the car. When Tess arrived, however, she was the one who got to keep Nina company and we reverted to the old policy of Brenin accompanying me everywhere.

Tess, being half wolf, was probably about half as destructive as the young Brenin would have been. But that was bad enough. She ate pretty much everything in the house. The valuable antique chairs bequeathed me by my grandmother didn't last more than a few weeks of her teething. The wall separating the kitchen from the utility room was a dry wall and she ate her way through that in a single afternoon – perhaps in a wholehearted but ultimately futile bid for the freedom of the back garden. She inherited the young Brenin's fondness for curtains. She also learned quite quickly how to open the cupboards in the kitchen in order to devour their contents – whether they were edible or not made little difference to her. When I put child-proof latches on the cupboards, she ate them too. Finally, she stopped messing around and ate the cupboards themselves. I lost the deeds to the house to one of these afternoon demolitions: Tess ate them. At least, I think it was Tess. Since there were two of them left at home, I could never really apportion blame with any confidence. But either way, I was screwed. I could hardly take the three of them into class with me.

When I got home in the evening, and after I had sifted

glumly through the wreckage of the afternoon's festivities, I would start writing. When I wrote, I would always have a bottle of Jack or Jim or Paddy on the go. And since I would generally write for around eight hours, it wasn't often that I would remember going to bed. The result was that after five years in Ireland, despite being drunk nearly every night, I had written six or seven books on topics ranging from the nature of the mind and consciousness through the value of nature to the rights of animals. Nor, apparently, were the books complete garbage. To my surprise, they were reviewed in all the good journals. And to my absolute astonishment, almost all the reviews were very positive. Institutions that wouldn't have touched me with a bargepole when I left Alabama now started to offer me jobs.

Initially, I resisted the idea of moving, since I didn't want to deprive Brenin and the girls of the countryside they loved so much. Eventually, however – since one extreme to the other seems to be a fairly constant theme in my life – I thought we would try London for a year and see how it went. I took a leave of absence from Cork and accepted an offer from Birkbeck College, University of London.

I was initially a little anxious about the practicalities of the move. Having read the last couple of pages, would you rent your house to me? Me: an alcoholic writer with three feral and hugely destructive canines in tow? You'd have to be mad. So the first rule of renting a house in London when you plan to move in with one and a half wolves and one and a half dogs is obvious: dissemble. 'Yeah, I have one small dog. Will that be OK?' It's not so much lying as the opposite of hyperbole – hypobole, if you like. It's understatement for effect – the effect being that you actually find someone who will rent their house to you. All right, it is lying. You then follow this up with some casual questions about the domicile of the landlord: 'Does the landlord live locally? Kenya? Right, I'll take it!'

So, just before Christmas, I put Brenin and the girls in the Jeep – Brenin and Tess in the back and Nina on the front seat, where she liked to be – and we took the ferry over to Britain, spent Christmas with my parents and drove on to London. Since the rather unfortunate episode with Brenin on Irish Ferries, I had switched allegiance to Stena, largely because they had large wooden kennels to put your dogs in during the voyage. Brenin, however, didn't like being put in a kennel during the voyage and generally registered his dissatisfaction by demolishing said kennel. Whenever I came down at the end of the crossing, he would invariably be running free over the car deck, to a chorus of yips and howls from the two girls, who had not been able to similarly extricate themselves. Once, a few trips after we had switched allegiance to Stena, I came down at the end of the voyage to find a grateful carpenter working on some of the damaged kennels. He was, apparently, delighted to meet the man who was throwing this extra work his way. And he summarized the overall situation quite accurately, I thought: 'I don't know why they don't allow him upstairs with you – he's cleaner than half the passengers!' In any event, as you might gather, I was looking forward to not having to make any more crossings for the foreseeable future. If I had, I'm pretty sure Stena would have banned us anyway.

I'd been over a few weeks previously, leaving Brenin and the girls with my parents for a day, and managed to find a little two-bedroomed cottage just a hop, skip and a jump from Wimbledon Common. I decided that the common's 1,100 acres of rolling countryside – or 4,000 acres of rolling countryside if you count the adjoining Richmond Park – simply teeming with small furry animals whose entire purpose in life was to be chased, would suit Brenin and the girls down to the ground. And it did.

We would go running on the common early every morning, because I needed to get them exhausted before I dared venture into work, through the alternating woodland and London Scottish golf course – possibly the only golf course in the world where dogs have the right of way. This was an approximately five-mile run, but Brenin and the girls ran at least three times that far. Whenever they saw a squirrel, they would tear off into the woods after it. Indeed, visual contact was not even required. A rustling in the undergrowth was enough to set them off. Happily, those squirrels are fast, and Brenin was slowing down. And neither Nina nor Tess ever really acquired his level of competence at hunting. So the squirrel and rabbit mortality associated with our daily excursion was very low. In fact, in our year there, I think they managed to kill only one squirrel – a level of collateral damage I thought acceptable in light of the immense enjoyment that it gave the three of them. After each chase, they'd bound back up to me, panting, eyes shining, and I'd say to them, 'Hey, is that any way for the dogs of the man who wrote *Animals Like Us* to behave!'

By the time we got back to the Jeep, all three of them were wrecked – but especially Brenin, who was now sliding gently from middle into old age. He would sleep most of the rest of the day. Taking him to classes with me wasn't really an option, since, at his age, I don't think he would have adjusted easily to the mysteries and vicissitudes of the London Underground. When I left the three of them at home together, I would give each of them a big cooked knucklebone that I'd purchased from the pet shop on the Broadway. This was a partial and temporary, relaxation of their piscetarian diet, driven by the overriding need to save the landlord's house from annihilation. Over the course of the year, it cost me a fortune – those knucklebones were around a fiver each – but was probably cheaper than buying the landlord a new kitchen. Incredibly, in the year we spent there, the girls did not inflict any damage on the house whatsoever. I had the carpets cleaned when we left and I swear you would not have known that any canines had been in residence. I don't know if this was because Nina and Tess had matured at just the right time. Or perhaps the knucklebones kept them entertained. Or perhaps Brenin kept them in line. Either way, I didn't ask any questions and just put it down to being lucky all my life.

So, mercifully, there was no arriving home to the usual tale of destruction or disaster. Once, I did arrive home to a deeply comic scene – which I came to call *the night of the three fat dogs*. The title was inaccurate, but rolled off the tongue better than the night of the two fat dogs and a fat wolf. It was my fault. At Birkbeck we taught classes only in the evenings. And, after class, I had (uncharacteristically) met a few friends at ULU – the University of London Students' Union bar – for a couple of quiet pints. I ended up getting the last tube home and arrived at some unspecified time after midnight. The three of them had managed to prise open the door to the pantry, where I kept the dog food. And they had worked their way through most of a twenty-kilogram bag of dry dog food. When I rolled in drunkenly, they tried to perform the usual dance of appeasement and placation – which they performed whenever they knew they had done something I wasn't going to be happy about. This involved trotting up to me, with their ears back and heads down, their noses low to the ground.

And they would wag their tails so exaggeratedly that it was really a body wag rather than a tail wag. Nina and Tess had been dancing this dance for most of their lives, on an almost daily basis. And Brenin himself was not unfamiliar with it. Tonight, however, it was a very different performance – the three of them were simply too fat to carry it off with any conviction. They tried to trot over to me, but could manage only a half-hearted stagger. They tried to perform the usual placatory body wag. But a body wag is a difficult thing to do when your body is as wide it is long – there's really nothing left to wag. Soon, they gave up and collapsed on the floor. If I was halfway sober, of course, I might have worried whether they had done themselves any permanent damage. But as it was, I just laughed and went to bed. The following morning, I said, 'Do you want to go for a walk?', the beginning of our daily ritual that they would respond to by cavorting around the house, howling and occasionally pushing me with their noses to make me go faster. For the first time ever there was no reaction. Heads remained firmly glued to the ground. They briefly lifted their eyes, but only, I think, to beseech me not to make them do anything in their current condition. I think what they were feeling that day was probably the closest thing to a canine hangover; and I could sympathize. So I let them sleep it off that day – not that they would have done the same thing for me if the positions had been reversed.

2

Jean-Michel was a jolly old man in his mid-sixties. Jean-Michel enjoyed life. He drank too much brandy and he smoked too many cigars. But perhaps his greatest enjoyment in life was fishing – that is how I met him; he used to fish the beach where I lived. When he arrived at work, he was invariably late, and not just a little late – he was always very late. But that didn't matter so much in the South of France, where tardiness is a way of life. And anyway, the business was his. That business was a veterinary practice in the city of Béziers. That I should have ever met Jean-Michel Audiquet was due to an entirely unexpected, and rather improbable, upturn in my fortunes. But, in the roller-coaster ride that has constituted my life, any such upturn has usually been followed by something rather nasty. This year would be no exception.

First, the good part. London hadn't really worked, largely due to my being both lazy and antisocial. I would teach my classes, but that was about it. I made no effort to get to know my new colleagues, or even show my face around the university, and quickly acquired the nickname 'the ghost'. However, I hadn't entirely misspent my time. While in London, I would split my writing up into two halves. I'd start around 7 p.m. For the first four or five hours I would write serious philosophy. By 'serious', I, of course, mean highly technical philosophy that probably only a few hundred people will ever read – in academia, if you can make it to a few thousand readers, you're a superstar. This is the sort of work that comes out in professional philosophical journals, or books that are published by university presses, such as Oxford, Cambridge and MIT. But for the second half of the evening, after midnight, when the Jack or Jim or Paddy had really started to kick in, I wrote something quite different. The result was a book called *The Philosopher at the End of the Universe* – an introduction to philosophy through the medium of blockbuster science-fiction films. Those of you who have read it will have no difficulty at all in believing that it was written in various stages of inebriation. However, to everyone's surprise – most of all that of the publishers – the book sold very well. In fact, money poured in from sales of foreign rights long before the book was even published. And so, not too long after my stint in London was over, I was unexpectedly sitting on a pile of cash – not a huge pile, but enough to keep me going for a while. Having no real idea what to do with it, but being fed up with the incessant rain – I swear it rained every single day I had lived in Ireland – I rented a house in the South of France and thought I would give full-time writing a go. And so we all moved down to a little house in the heart of Languedoc.

The house was on the edge of a village. Bordering it was an absolutely stunning nature reserve made up of the coastal delta of the River Orb. The reserve was part saltwater lagoon: the *maïre*, as it was called there – an Occitan word synonymous, and roughly homonymous, with the English word 'mire'. And the area was swarming with the black bulls, white ponies and pink flamingos characteristic of the region. Every morning, we would walk down through the reserve to the beach and go for a swim. I thought Brenin and the girls would take to the French lifestyle, and I wasn't wrong.

However, a month or so after we moved, Brenin became ill. I'd noticed a general lethargy which started, in hindsight, even before we left London. At first, I put it down to him becoming old. But when he started declining his evening meal, so much so that I had to coax him to eat it, I took him straight to the vet – the only vet, and one of the few people, I knew in France: Jean-Michel Audiquet. I wasn't particularly looking forward to this visit. Jean-Michel didn't speak a word of English, and in those days my schoolboy French really wasn't up to the demands of a medical consultation, even if it was only veterinary medicine. But I never imagined there would be anything seriously wrong. I thought he would tell me that Brenin was simply old, and it was hot, and of course he didn't want to eat as much as before.

Luckily, however, Jean-Michel took his work very seriously. We arrived at 11 a.m. on a Wednesday and he had blood tests done by 11.15. Brenin was under the knife at 11.30. In his examination, Jean-Michel had been able to feel a lump in Brenin's abdominal area. The lump turned out to be a tumour on his spleen, one that had, he told me, been close to rupturing. He removed Brenin's spleen – apparently you can live OK without one – and I went home in a state of shock. But incredibly, by the evening, Brenin was back on his feet, if a little unsteadily, and I was able to go back in and bring him home. Jean-Michel told me that he had not been able to see any other signs of cancer and with any luck it would prove to be a primary not secondary tumour. The blood tests would be back in a week or so and we would know more then. I was to take him home, let him rest and bring him back in two days' time.

With Jean-Michel, you could always tell when the treatment was going well, or at least seemed to be going well, because then he would let himself engage in another of his favourite pastimes: *blaguing*. French not being one of my strong suits, most things would go straight over the top of my head, and so his jokes at my expense could never afford to be either subtle or clever. He would fix me with a serious stare and say, solemnly, '*Ce n'est pas bon.*' It's not good. He would shake his head. But then he would look at me again, break into a broad grin and say, '*C'est très bon!*' It's very good! And, of course, because my French was bad, and I was concentrating so hard on processing what he was saying, I would fall for it every time.

It was just after our return, two days after the surgery, that the complications began to appear. I drove back from the vet's feeling a little happier than I had for a few days. Jean-Michel had been very positive and I was starting to hope that everything might turn out OK. Brenin was ten years old now and I knew he wasn't going to be around for too much longer. But I wasn't ready to lose him yet — as if I was ever going to be ready for that. But I was starting to hope that maybe he could dodge this particular bullet.

Back at the house, when I helped him out of the Jeep, I noticed his rear end was covered in blood. I rushed him straight back to the vet's. One of Brenin's anal glands had become infected, a circumstance neither I nor Jean-Michel noticed until blood started pouring out of it. So now Brenin had to suffer the further indignity of having his rump shaved. Then Jean-Michel cut open the anal gland to allow the infection to drain out. Brenin was put on a cocktail of antibiotics and I took him home again. It was there that the real horror began.

It is of vital importance, Jean-Michel informed me, that the area is kept clean. And this meant that I had to wash Brenin's bum every two hours with warm water and something that, according to my translation, he referred to as 'feminine soap'. Apparently it's a French thing — but you can get it at any chemist. So, that was another thing on my list of things I was really looking forward to doing: going to the village pharmacy and asking, perhaps with some supplementary miming should my vocabulary or grammar fail me, the rather attractive woman behind the counter whether she had any feminine soap. After I'd thoroughly scrubbed poor old Brenin's backside, I had to syringe the anal gland. That is, I had to take a syringe, fill it with an antibacterial solution, stick it in Brenin's now open and suppurating anal gland and inject him. And I had to do this every two hours, day and night. The key to his recovery, I was told, was making sure that the infection in the anal gland didn't cross over and infect his surgery wound.

Jean-Michel told me to bring him in the following day. This I did, after a night of absolutely no sleep. By the time I reached the office, Brenin's other anal gland had gone too and there was blood pouring out everywhere. '*Mon Dieu*,' said Jean-Michel, and repeated the procedure of yesterday – he shaved the rest of Brenin's bottom and cut open the other gland. I returned home for a long weekend of double-duty washing and syringing: every two hours, day and night. Nor was I to get much sleep between syringings either. Brenin had a big plastic surgical collar on, to prevent him from licking first one wound and then the other. Obviously, he detested this, and his preferred method of registering this was by slamming the collar against walls, tables, televisions and anything else he encountered.

Brenin was not, of course, happy about the treatment he was receiving. From his point of view, he went into the vet's on Wednesday, feeling merely mildly unwell, and now he was having atrocity after atrocity inflicted on him every two hours. And, although he was not as strong as usual, he was still pretty strong and wasn't going to allow me to interfere with his rear end if he could possibly help it. So I had to advance on him, corner him and drag him by the collar over to where I had left the bowl of soapy water, sponge and syringe. Then I had to force him to the ground, lie across him while he struggled and, when he got too weak to struggle, begin the washing and syringing. While I did this, Brenin would just lie there and whimper. Listening to that whimpering was one of the hardest things I've ever had to do.

When I took Brenin back into the vet's on what I came to call Black Monday – which followed Black Friday, when his first anal gland went, and Black Saturday, when his second one turned also – his surgery wound had become cross-infected with the infection from the anal glands. He was now a very, very sick wolf. The cocktail of antibiotics that Jean-Michel had prescribed wasn't working. On Friday, Jean-Michel had taken a swab and sent it away to a lab for testing, to find out which sort of bacterial infection it was and, more importantly, which antibiotics it was sensitive to. However, the results weren't due back for a few days. In the meantime, we tried another antibiotic – efloroxacine – which had proved successful against highly resistant strains in the past. Also, Jean-Michel had to reopen Brenin's surgery wound to scoop out the infection. The cleaning and syringing of his bottom continued apace, every two hours, for the next couple of days. But I now also had to do the same for his stomach, though, of course, with a different syringe.

When I brought him in again on Wednesday, the news was bad but not entirely unexpected. Brenin had a highly antibiotic-resistant form of *E. coli* similar in many ways to MRSA. The bacteria had, presumably, been in his gut prior to the surgery and his weakened immune system had allowed it to run riot. The upshot was that he was almost certainly going to die.

In a last throw of the dice, Jean-Michel decided to try something old school, something that really wasn't done any more in the age of antibiotics. You've heard of people having knee reconstructions and shoulder reconstructions. Well, poor old Brenin had what was, in effect, an arse reconstruction.

Noticing that his bum was reeking of bacteria, despite being spotless, and noticing the swelling in the area below the anal glands, Jean-Michel decided that Brenin's problem now was that evolution had been less than maximally efficient in the doling out of anal glands. They might be very good for storing up scent for marking territory, but they were far less effective at draining unwanted bacterial infections. So Jean-Michel once more put Brenin under the knife and, if my translational abilities did not lead me astray, moved his anal glands an inch or so south (and you can imagine the amount of miming, by both parties, and the number of sketches that had to be drawn, to successfully communicate this idea to me). I was not too clear on the details or the mechanics, but the idea, Jean-Michel told me, was that the infection would now nat-urally drain out rather than being bottled up. But he – and I – didn't hold out much hope.

3

I picked Brenin up again that evening and took him home to die. It is difficult to convey the sense of isolation, loneliness and desperation of those days. The real horror lay not in the realization that I was going to lose Brenin. All lives come to an end and – but for the six months he had spent incarcer-ated – I was happy with the life he had led. I believe he was too. The horror of the situation lay in doing what I had to do in order to try and keep him alive. Of course, his wounds were disgusting: they reeked of decay, and the stench of this permeated the entire house. But the horror had nothing to do with this. The horror lay in the suffering I had to impose on Brenin: suffering I had to inflict on him every two hours;

suffering that would almost certainly be futile. At the core of this suffering, I think, was a certain kind of loneliness. This was not my loneliness – that was irrelevant. It was the loneliness of my boy.

Brenin was terrified – and all my efforts at comforting him could not change this. It is likely also that he was in significant pain – although I was not certain of this. But I am certain that my cleaning of his wounds, which I was still doing every two hours, day and night, hurt him considerably. My efforts to clean and heal him were inevitably accompanied by anything ranging from faint whimpering to high-decibel screeching. I believed that I was losing Brenin's love. That was a horrible thought, but it did not get us to the heart of the present situation. If Brenin could only get better, I would be quite content with him hating me for the rest of his life. That is one of the many bargains that I, in my sleep-deprived psychosis, struck with God. The shit had indeed hit the fan, but my wolf cub was now old and dying in front of me. The real horror was the idea that Brenin would think he had lost my love. I kept thinking that he would remember the last few days of his life as ones where he was tortured by the man who was supposed to love him. I had betrayed him, abandoned him. And I was not the only one. Nina and Tess were frightened by Brenin's big plastic collar. Whenever he went over to where they were lying, they would get up and go to the other side of the room. This broke my heart, and I think a little piece of it will always remain broken. People often say – usually when they're trying to be dramatic – that we all die alone. Whether this is true, I don't know. But, while it is easy to anthropomorphize these sorts of situations, it is difficult to avoid the conclusion that Brenin must have felt utterly alone, betrayed, abandoned and even brutalized by the pack that had been his life.

I am a *consequentialist* about matters moral. I believe that the rightness or wrongness of an action is solely a matter of its consequences. I am one of those people who believe that the road to hell is paved with good intentions. I've always had a deep distrust of intentions. I think that intentions are often masks, and masks within masks: pretences that we use to disguise the ugly truth of our real motivation. I told myself I would do for Brenin whatever I would want someone to do for me in similar circumstances. I wouldn't keep him alive just for the sake of it, because I wouldn't want to be kept alive just for the sake of it. But, if there was hope that I could recover and lead a full and fulfilling life, then I would want someone to fight for me – even if I didn't understand what they were doing. And so, I told myself, I should fight for Brenin – even if he didn't understand what I was doing, and even if he didn't want me to do it. That is what I told myself, over and over again. But perhaps in reality, I simply wasn't ready – wasn't yet strong enough – to face a life without Brenin. Perhaps my seemingly noble principle – do unto Brenin as you would want others to do unto you – was just a mask to hide my unreadiness. Who knows what my real motivation was? Who knows if there is even any such thing as a real motivation? And, quite frankly, who cares?

In forcing Brenin to suffer like this, and in all likelihood to die like this, I was wagering my consequentialist soul. I was making the single most constant and important figure in my life over the past decade die a death that was full of pain and fear; a death where he felt abandoned by those he loved. If Brenin died, my actions would have been unpardonable. There would be no forgiveness for me for what I had done – and nor should there be. On the other hand, what if I had simply given up? What if I had given up when Brenin could have recovered? We cling so hard to our intentions, I think, because consequences are so unforgiving. Consequences damn us if we do; and frequently they also damn us if we don't. For us consequentialists, it is often only luck – dumb luck – that can save us.

4

Brenin got better: incredible, but true. After a month or so – the precise timeline is something on which I was never too clear – I woke up from a few snatched minutes of sleep and there was something different about him. I couldn't put my finger on it, but something had changed. I now realize that it was this: Brenin was looking at me. I now understand that in the last month he had been averting his eyes from me – perhaps because he thought that if he caught my gaze I would remember that I should be in the process of inflicting pain on him. But I didn't know this at the time. My first thought was this was it. I had seen both dogs and people die before, and I knew that often the immediate hours before they die are marked by an apparent recovery – just for a few hours they seem to be getting stronger, but this is only a sign that they are about to slip away. But Brenin didn't slip away. In the next few days, his recovery continued, spreading throughout his body like a whispered rumour through a crowd, a rumour that slowly but surely transformed before my eyes into a promise. His appetite grew and his strength slowly returned. In a week's time, we were ready for our first walk in well over a month – a gentle stroll into the reserve to look at the flamingos. The washing and syringing of the wounds, of course, continued, and would for several weeks. But the infection was broken. And Brenin no longer objected to my ministrations; he now just lay there patiently until I did what had to be done.

When I look back on those days, it is with a pronounced sense of unreality. For more than a month, the exigencies of Brenin's treatment permitted me almost no sleep. Exhaustion would sometimes make me drop off, but I think this was only ever for a few minutes. Sometimes, when I woke, I would have forgotten that Brenin was ill. But then I would notice the stench of decay in my nostrils, and the situation, in its horror and hopelessness, would reassert itself over my consciousness. After even a few days of this, the delusions – the delusions of sleep deprivation – kick in. There were several, but the most common one was that I was dead and in hell, and this was it for all eternity.

Tertullian, the most vicious and depraved of the early Christians – and that is saying something – had a preferred vision of hell as a place where all those who were not saved were tortured by demons who would stick red-hot pitchforks in their bottoms, and things like that. The saved, on the other hand, would be in heaven's box seats, laughing down gleefully at the torments of the damned. It is difficult to feel anything but contempt for Tertullian and the depths of the resentment he must have harboured for him to think of heaven and hell in these terms. Heaven was a spiteful place for Tertullian, and this was nothing more than a reflection of his spiteful soul. But as for hell, I think Tertullian's vision is pretty mild.

Hell would be far worse if it were not a place where you are tortured and brutalized but, rather, a place where you are forced to torture and brutalize those you love most. You are forced to do this even though you find it sickening and this revulsion permeates through you to the depths of your soul. You are forced to do it even though it will cost you the thing you value most in the world: their love. But you do it anyway because – and here we find the genius of hell – it is for their own good. Hell gives you the choice and you do it anyway because the alternative is worse. This is far worse than Tertullian's hell. If I were in this hell, I would exchange places with Tertullian's damned in a heartbeat. In those days when Brenin was dying, I used to think this was what hell was – being forced to torture a wolf I loved because it was for his own good. But this would be a strange hell, in the same way that Tertullian's vision was of a strange heaven. Tertullian's heaven was populated with people who hate. My hell would be populated with people who love. I would like to think that those who hate can never go to heaven, and those who love can never go to hell. But the consequentialist in me won't let me believe this.

5

People say all the time that they love their dogs. And I'm sure they think they do. But, believe me, until you've cleaned your dog's smelly, suppurating, disease-ridden arse every two hours for well over a month, you really don't know. We usually think of love as a sort of warm, fuzzy feeling. But love has many faces and this was just one of them.

When Brenin was so ill, I was the subject of a *mélange*, a haphazard assortment, of feelings, emotions and desires, none constant or prominent enough to be called the feeling of love. Much of the time, I felt as if I had been smashed in the face – breathless, shaky, dizzy, nauseous. Much of the time, I felt as if I was walking in, or rather through, quicksand; as if the air had partially congealed around me into a thick viscous stew that made any spontaneous action, or even thought, impossible. Mostly, I just felt numb. At one point, when I was certain he was going to die – and I don't like to admit this, but it is true – I felt almost relieved, and thought that if, when I next went over to wash and syringe him, he didn't wake up, then maybe that was for the best.

Feelings, feelings, feelings: all of them powerful, some almost overwhelming. But none of them that could be plausibly identified with the love I had for Brenin. The love in question is what Aristotle would have called *philia*. This is the love of the family, the love of the pack. It is distinguished from *eros* – the passionate longing of erotic love – and *agape* – the impersonal love of God and humanity as a whole. My attachment to Brenin was, I assure you, in no way erotic. And nor did I love Brenin in the way that the Bible tells me I should love my neighbour or love my God. I loved Brenin as a brother. And this love – this *philia* – is not a feeling of any sort.

Feelings can be manifestations of *philia*, and they can accompany it; but they are not what *philia* is. Why did I feel numb and nauseous? How could I actually feel relieved by the prospect of Brenin's imminent death? Because I loved Brenin, and making him suffer so much was almost – but thank God not quite – unbearable. These feelings – diverse, disparate and disunited though they may be – are all manifestations of this love. But love is not any of these feelings. There are so many feelings that can, in different contexts, accompany it that *philia* cannot be identified with any of them. And it can exist without any of them.

Love has many faces. And if you love, you have to be

strong enough to look upon all of them. The essence of *philia* is, I think, far harsher, far crueller, than we care to admit. There is one thing without which *philia* cannot exist; and this is not a matter of feeling but of the will. *Philia* – the love appropriate to your pack – is the will to do something for those who are of your pack, even though you desperately don't want to do it, even though it horrifies and sickens you, and even though you may ultimately have to pay a very high price for it, perhaps heavier than you can bear. You do this because that is what is best for them. You do this because you must. You may never have to do this. But you must always be ready to do it. Love is sometimes sickening. Love can damn you for all eternity. Love will take you to hell. But if you are lucky, if you are very lucky, it will bring you back again.

8

Time's Arrow

1

The last thing I ever said to Brenin was: we'll meet again in dreams. I said it as the vet inserted the hypodermic needle into a vein on his front right leg – I remember the leg, I remember the vein – and injected a lethal amount of anaesthetic into his body. By the time I had completed the sentence, he was gone. I'd like to think he wasn't there anyway. I'd like to think he was in Alabama, nuzzling up in his mother's fur. I'd like to think he was in Knockduff with Nina and Tess, leaping through the seas of barley as the diffident Irish sun rose on a scene of misty golden splendour. I'd like to think he was with them again on Wimbledon Common, crashing through the woods in pursuit of squirrels and those rascally rabbits. And I'd like to think he was with them again, splashing through the warm Mediterranean surf.

The cancer that had announced itself with his illness of a

year ago had returned, this time metastasized and irredeemably malign. It was a lymphosarcoma, which is treatable in humans but, the vicissitudes of veterinary science being what they are, almost always results in death in dogs. I decided against any invasive attempts to save him this time, because I really don't think he would have survived surgery, let alone any more post-surgical complications. I was shocked to discover that, in the year since Brenin's illness, Jean-Michel, the vet whose old-school expertise had saved him last time, had already gone – also the victim of cancer. And when the vet who had taken over the practice told me this, I think I sensed Brenin's time was up too.

I kept him as comfortable as I could, and for the first time in his life I let him sleep on the bed with me – to the immense chagrin of Nina and Tess, who couldn't believe I was excluding them from this appealing and unprecedented treat. When the painkillers stopped working and his pain – in my honest, agonized but deeply fallible judgement – became too great, I drove him into Béziers to be killed. And there he died, in the back of the same sort of Jeep in which we had driven all around the south-eastern United States all those years ago – in search of rugby and parties and women and beer.

I couldn't bury him in the garden – the owners of the house would almost certainly have taken exception to that. So I buried him at a place where we stopped every day on our walks, a small clearing surrounded by beech trees and scrub oak. The ground was sandy and it didn't take me long to dig a substantial hole. When I had put Brenin in the ground, I built over his grave a cairn, made from rocks I carried across from the *digue*: the dyke that prevented the winter storm surges from sweeping up into the village. This was a long and arduous process, as the *digue* was a couple of hundred yards away, and it took me well into the night to finish the job. Then I lit a driftwood bonfire and decided to sit with my brother through the rest of the night.

This is the part of the story that I am reluctant to tell, since – once again – I come across as completely psychotic, which I no doubt was. Keeping me company were Nina and Tess, and two litres of Jack Daniel's, which I had stockpiled knowing that this night was coming soon. I had been dry for the past few weeks, since I needed to keep my mind clear to make the best decisions I could for Brenin. I couldn't afford to have any alcohol-induced melancholy make me send him on his way a moment before his time; nor could I allow any alcohol-induced euphoria to force him to cling to this life when it was not worth living. It was the first time in years that I had been dry for more than a day or two, and I planned on decisively breaking that drought tonight. And so, after Brenin had been taken care of, Nina and Tess lay quietly by the fire and listened to my bourbon-fuelled rage against the dying of the light. By the time I was significantly into my second litre, what had started out as a quiet rumination about the possibility of an afterlife had transformed into a raging torrent of invective directed against God. It went something like this: Come on then, you f*****g c**t! You show me. If we live on, you f****r, show me now!

The next bit sounds horrendously far-fetched, but I swear to God it's true. At the very moment I said this, I looked across the fire and saw him: I saw Brenin's ghost of stone.

I want to emphasize just how inexplicable this is. When I made the cairn, I travelled up and down the *digue*, picking up rocks wherever I found them detached or loose. Then I carried them back a couple of hundred yards or so to the clearing. When I got there, I simply dropped them on Brenin's grave. I repeated this many, many times, and the entire process took around five hours. The dropping of the rocks on the grave was an entirely random process. I am still convinced of this. I didn't place the stones, I just dropped them. I had no overall vision of the completed cairn driving me on. On the contrary, I just wanted it finished, and I wanted to get astonishingly drunk.

But now – there – staring back at me through the flames was Brenin's ghost of stone. The front of the cairn was his head: a diamond-shaped slab of rock, snout resting, as was his fashion, on the ground; and with a stain of moss on the sharp end that looked, for the world, like his nose. The rest of the cairn was a wolf curled up as if in the snow – a habit inculcated in Brenin by his Arctic forebears, and which he found difficult to break, even in the heat of an Alabama or Languedoc summer. There, at the zenith of my rage and need, he stared back at me.

Depth psychologists – Freudians, Jungians and their ilk – might say that I unconsciously created the image of a sleeping Brenin; my dropping of the stones on his grave was guided by an unconscious desire to create a monument to him in his image. Perhaps they are right, but the explanation strikes me as deeply implausible. It doesn't explain the prominent role played by chance in the construction of the cairn. When I had carried a rock back to the mound, I didn't place it there; I dropped it, and immediately turned and set off in search of the next one. Some rocks stayed where they were dropped, but most didn't; they rolled to the lowest available point. If they rolled, and where they rolled to, were matters of chance. And this is why the depth-psychological story falls short. It is one thing for my unconscious to control my actions, but it is quite another for my unconscious to control chance itself.

It would be easy to explain Brenin's stone ghost as an alcohol-induced hallucination or confabulation. It would be even easier to think of it as a dream. We shall indeed meet again in dreams. But Brenin's stone ghost never left. I fell asleep on the ground by the fire, and perhaps would have frozen to death as the fire died, but for a fortuitous bout of vomiting that forced me to wake up. But Brenin's stone ghost was still there when I awoke. It is still there today.

2

Brenin's last year was a gift for both of us. I remember that year as a season of never-ending summer. I've never been one to obsessively keep track of time. I lost my last watch in a poker game in Charleston, South Carolina, back in 1992 and I haven't got around to replacing it yet. Not having a timepiece is, of course, scarcely liberation from the constraints of time – I seem to spend half my life asking people what the time is. But the best thing about living in France was that it was the nearest thing to a timeless existence I have been able to experience or imagine. There, we lived not by the clock, but by the sun. Actually, who am I kidding? We did live by a clock, but it was Nina's clock, not my own.

I would arise at sun-up – in the summer that was around 6 in the morning. I would know it was sun-up, because that was Nina's signal to get up and start licking whatever hand or foot of mine was exposed outside the bedsheet. And if no hand or foot was exposed outside the sheet, she would rearrange the sheet with her nose until there was. I would make my way rather gingerly down the steep pine staircase – my sluggish early-morning wariness the result of a blown-out knee from my rugby days – laptop in hand. I would sit on the terrace at the front of the house and write during the misty mosquitoed cool of the early morning. Brenin would lie over in the northern corner of the garden, curled up as in snow, with his snout stretching along the ground. Nina, the pack's timekeeper, would lie by the gate, beady eyes always on me, waiting for the promised walk that still lay a few hours off. Tess, the pack's princess, would wait until I was immersed in my writing, and then glide silently back into the house, to see if she could sneak on to my bed without me realizing – which she usually could.

Then, around 10, before it became too hot, Nina would get up, come over to me and put her head in my lap. If this didn't have the desired reaction – me desisting in my typing – she would flick her snout up sharply and repeatedly into my forearms, making further typing impossible. The message was unequivocal: time to go to the beach. This was not so much a stroll as a military operation. First, there was the preliminary rounding up of parasols and other beach paraphernalia such as balls and/or Frisbees. This would inform the other members of the pack of our impending march, and the result was a chorus of howls, yips and barks that signalled to everyone in the village that we were on the move. The Frisbee was for Nina, an enthusiastic and accomplished swimmer. The parasols were for Brenin and Tess. They would paddle and sometimes, on breathless days when the sea was calm and clear, they could be coaxed into swimming properly. But they never really enjoyed it – they would swim out to me, tension bordering on panic clearly visible on their faces, but when they reached me they would immediately turn around and swim back to the beach. That was where they preferred to spend most of their time. When I became tired of watching them panting away in the increasingly hot sun, I invested in a couple of parasols, one each. Looking back, I now understand that by this time in my life I must have been becoming a little 'peculiar' – an old woman with lots of cats sort of peculiar. On the plus side, the numerous thieves that populated southern French beaches during the summer months always gave our pitch a wide birth. As did the other dogs.

During the walk to the beach, there were certain things that had to be done in a certain order and manner. The neighbourhood dogs were greeted and, where necessary, intimidated in the appropriate fashion: first Vanille, the female English setter, to be intimidated by Nina, with Tess acting as sidekick, but greeted in a friendly if somewhat aloof way by Brenin; then Rouge, the big male ridgeback, to have his garden fence urinated on by Brenin, but to be met with an enthusiasm that bordered on gushing by both Nina and Tess; and finally the female Dogo Argentino that I mentioned earlier, but whose name I never discovered, who once made the mistake of attacking Tess. Accordingly, Tess singled her out for special treatment: she would store up her first bowel movement of the morning until we reached the dog's house and then would deposit it as near as was humanly – or rather caninely – possible to the garden fence. Thinking about it now, perhaps that is why the Dogo always tried to bite me.

Tess was, in general, a master of the tactical deployment of faeces. Once, when we lived in Wimbledon and were walking across the golf-course part of the common, she actually managed, in a display of breathtaking accuracy, to poo directly on top of a golf ball that had landed nearby. My advice, 'If I were you I would take the drop', did little to mollify the partly enraged but mostly incredulous member of London Scottish Golf Club.

After the last of the houses, we would enter the vineyards – or rather, the failed vineyards, long since abandoned to the salty ground and frequent storm surges. Through the vineyards and on to the *maïre*, which ran from the *digue* down to the beach at its northern end. At the right times of the year, the *maïre* would be carpeted in pink flamingos – the *flamants roses*, as they are known in the far more beautiful French language. If one happened to stray on to the shore, Nina and Tess would make sure it was given a good chase until it flew away back to its own legitimate domain. Thankfully, neither of them ever came remotely close to catching one. While they chased ineffectually, Brenin would give me a look as if to say, 'The youth of today. If I were a few years younger . . .'

Once we reached the beach, Nina would make a beeline for the water and start bouncing around, loudly demanding her Frisbee. There was a strict 'No dogs' policy on the beach during the summer – although the policy didn't actually mention wolves per se. But the French, of course, are well known for taking the laws of their land as a series of suggestions rather than requirements; the law was rarely enforced and the beach was typically carpeted with dogs. The *gendarmes* would turn up occasionally and make a show of fining people, but whenever we saw them we would head off down the beach away from them, safe in the knowledge that they would never walk far. We did get caught a few times, however – an annoyance that had less to do with the amount of the fine and more to do with the length of the lecture you would be required to listen to before they fined you. Through a combination of luck, stealth and feigned gormlessness, we managed to negotiate the entire summer with fines totalling no more than 100 euros or so.

After the beach and just before everything closed for lunch – again, it was Nina who would let us know when it was time to go – we would walk over to the village and the *boulangerie*. I would divide up a couple of *pains au chocolat* between the three of them. This division always took place according to a clearly defined ritual. We would leave the *boulangerie* and walk over to the stone bench a few yards in front of the shop. I would sit, open the paper bag and tear off bits of the *pain*, feeding them in turn to each of them, while trying to avoid the copious amounts of saliva flying in my general direction. Swimming is hungry work. Following that, we would head over to Yvette's bar, where I would have an inadvisably large number of glasses of rosé – the daytime drink of choice in Languedoc – while the dog-loving Yvette gave them a bowl of water and made a big fuss of Brenin. Then we would walk home, around the back of the village and down through the woodlands that bordered the house.

When we arrived home, we would all find ourselves shadows in which to spend the heat of the day. I would again write. At this time of day, the inside of the house was far too hot for Tess's liking, so she used to lie at my feet under the table on the terrace. Nina preferred the far wall on that terrace, shaded for most of the day by the terrace's roof. The northern part of the garden now being in sunshine, Brenin would head upstairs to the sun terrace, seeking out its shady corner. This gave him a fine view of the surrounding countryside and, more importantly, an early view of anything of interest that was approaching. We'd begin to stir when the shadows grew long, around 7. First, I would make dinner for the four-legged ones. Then a few aperitifs for the two-legged one. Then we would go for a walk, one which would typically culminate at La Réunion, our favourite restaurant.

I say 'our', rather than 'my', favourite restaurant advisedly. I went there for my dinner. Brenin and the girls went there for their second dinner. Lionel and Martine, the proprietors, always saved us one of the big round tables in the corner, where there was plenty of room for the dogs to stretch out. I would make my way slowly through a four-course meal, and the animals would levy certain not insignificant taxes on each course. As everyone who has lived in France will know, it is impossible to be a vegetarian there – certainly not in country France. When I first mentioned my dietary restrictions to Lionel, he looked at me uncomprehendingly and suggested chicken. Consequently, I had, at this time, followed Brenin and the girls and become a piscetarian. I would typically start with the St Jacques salad, since it was utterly magnificent and would contain anything up to ten scallops. Three of those would go to the canine contingent. Following that, three strips of the smoked salmon would be levied from the second course. Most of the skin, tail and head of the *sole meunière* that often followed would similarly be siphoned off from the third course. And I would get a free extra crêpe to divide up between them when I had the final course – Lionel's kind contribution to the evening's canine fare. Of course, I kept the wine and the *marc de muscat* – a type of brandy made from the muscat grape – to myself. We would walk gently home after that, following the edge of the *digue* – me pleasantly drunk and my canine friends pleasantly full. We always slept well.

That was every summer's day during the last year of

Brenin's life. And it is a long and beautiful summer in Languedoc. The winter, of course, forced on us certain adjustments. Tragically, La Réunion was closed between mid-November and mid-March – Lionel and Martine worked the ski resorts during those months. There was also less swimming involved – certainly by me if not Nina. Nina allowed me to sleep in until around 8 a.m. And my early-morning writing was done largely indoors. My midday sojourn in Yvette's tended to last somewhat longer – since I didn't have anywhere to go in the evenings. But the basic outline of the day – the day's essence – was the same.

Through all of this – summer and winter – it was Nina who was the keeper of time. In this, she was driven on by something that happened fairly early during our stay in France – an event so dark and tragic that, even now, years later, I suspect it still haunts her. It was my fault and I take full responsibility. I don't know if I spent just a little too long at my laptop that day, or maybe I tarried just a little too long in the comforting cool waters of the Mediterranean. Whatever the reason, when we arrived at the village that day . . . the *boulangerie* had closed for lunch. And it is a long and beautiful lunch in Languedoc.

Of course, objectively – and it's easy for me to take this attitude – it wasn't really that much of a big deal. I just had to spend an hour or so longer than usual in Yvette's – which I happily did – and the *boulangerie* would be open again at 4 p.m. But looking at food-related issues objectively has never been one of Nina's strengths. Nor has delay of gratification. The hours she spent in Yvette's that day were ones of agonized confusion, existential angst of the most debilitating sort (it goes without saying that Yvette's bar didn't do food). She paced up and down the entire time, a crazed glint in her eyes. This was not how it was supposed to be. This was the long, dark lunchtime of her soul.

Come 4 p.m., of course, the world all made sense again and the day could resume its normal course. But after that day, Nina was motivated by twin fears: the fear of the *boulangerie* being closed by the time she arrived and the fear of not going to La Réunion. God forbid I should ever take a different route to that restaurant in the evening. As soon as we got within a few hundred yards of it, she was going anyway, whether the rest of us came or not.

It wasn't until afterwards – after Brenin had died and I had moved away from France – that I really understood just how intensely uniform this year of my life had been. But I suppose it was just a continuation of the sort of life we had enjoyed in Ireland and London. Almost everyone I know would describe this life – its regularity and repetition – as monotonous, even boring in the extreme. But I think I learned more from those days than perhaps from anyone or anything. The key to what I learned is to be found in a deceptively simple question: what did Brenin lose when he died?

3

It should be pretty clear that I – a madman howling at the moon and raging at God – lost a lot when Brenin died. And people will tell you – as they have told me – that this was a function of the sad and solitary life I led during those years. Maybe that's true. But I'm not interested in what I lost; I'm interested in what he lost.

In what sense is death a bad thing? Not for other people, but for the person who dies? In what sense would your death be a bad thing for you? Death, whatever else it is, is not something that occurs in a life. Wittgenstein once said that his life had no limit in the way that his visual field had no limit. Obviously, he didn't mean that we live for ever – Wittgenstein himself died, also of cancer, in 1951. Rather, he was pointing out that death is the limit of a life; and the limit of a life is not something that can occur in that life any more than the limit of a visual field is something that can occur in that field. The limit of a visual field is not something you see: you are aware of it precisely because of what you don't see. This is how it is with limits: a limit of something is not part of that thing – if it was, then it wouldn't be the limit of it.

If we accept this, then we are immediately faced with a problem: it seems that death cannot be harmful to the person who dies. The classic version of the problem was stated, 2,000 years before Wittgenstein, by the ancient Greek philosopher Epicurus. Death, Epicurus argued, cannot harm us. While we are alive, death has not happened and so can't have harmed us yet. And when we die – since death is the limit of our life and not an event in it – we are no longer around for it to harm. Therefore death cannot be a bad thing, at least not for the person who dies.

What is wrong with Epicurus's argument? Indeed, is there anything wrong with it? Among humans at least, there is near-universal consensus that there is something wrong with it. And there also appears to be substantial agreement on why it is wrong: death harms us because of what it takes away. Death is what philosophers call a harm of deprivation. That, however, is the easy part. The hard part lies in understanding what it takes from us, and how it can take anything from us when we are no longer around to have anything taken.

We will not get very far in answering these questions by saying that death harms us because it takes away our life. For if Wittgenstein is right, and death is the limit of our life, and so does not occur within our life, then a life is precisely what we do not have when death happens to us. But we can only have something taken from us if we actually have that thing. So how can death take something from us that we no longer have?

A more promising answer, I think, is possibilities. Death harms us because it takes away all of our possibilities. But, in the end, I don't think this idea is going to work either. Part of the problem is that possibilities are too promiscuous; there are far too many possibilities, and so nothing in a possibility that makes it intrinsically mine or yours. Among the possibilities I have are ones in which I take no interest whatsoever. It is possible that I will become a tinker, tailor, soldier or sailor; it is possible that I will become a beggarman or thief. But I have no interest in following up on, or trying to realize, any of these possibilities. It is possible that I will die tomorrow, or in fifty years' time. But I have far more interest in trying to realize the latter possibility than the former. Possibilities just come too cheap. Each one of us has an infinite – or at least a huge and indefinite – number of possibilities. And we are only interested in realizing a tiny fraction of those. Indeed, we are not even aware of most of our possibilities.

More than that, many of our possibilities are ones that we fervently hope will never be realized. Most of us are probably not too keen on following up on the beggarman/thief possibilities. It is possible that any one of us might become a murderer, torturer, paedophile, madman or madwoman. Something is possible if there is no contradiction involved in supposing that it happens: that is the definition of a possibility. So, no matter how unlikely you think it is that any of these possibilities will be realized, they are still possibilities. Some of our possibilities we hope will come true. But some of them we pray will never come true. Among our possibilities are ones that we would embrace and others that we would reject in the strongest possible terms. I doubt that death can harm us by depriving us of possibilities in which we have no interest. And I'm certain that it can't harm us by depriving us of possibilities we would reject with every fibre of our being. In the case of some possibilities, we would rather die than see them realized. Death cannot harm us by depriving us of those.

However, the concept of possibilities does point us in the direction of a more promising account. It is only some of our possibilities that are relevant to the harm of death: those we hope are realized or come true. To each of these possibilities there corresponds a desire: a desire for the possibility to be realized. If we are serious about this desire, but we can't satisfy it immediately, then we might find ourselves making it a goal to satisfy this desire. And if this goal is a difficult one to achieve, we might find ourselves engaging much of our energy and time in a project for achieving this goal. It is, I think, in terms of the concepts of desire, goal and project that we humans will inevitably try to understand why death is a bad thing for the person who dies.

It might seem as if we have made no headway against Epicurus's problem. If death is the limit of a life, and not something that occurs in a life, by the time it happens we are no longer around to be deprived of anything – including desires, goals and projects. However, desires, goals and projects all have something in common, something that is crucial to Epicurus's problem. They are all what we might call future-directed: in their very nature they direct us beyond the present time towards the future. It is because we have desires, goals and projects that we have a future: a future is something that each of us has now, at the present time. Death harms us by depriving us of a future.

4

The idea of losing a future is, when you think about it, a very strange one. And its strangeness comes from the strangeness of the idea of the future. The future does not yet exist. So how can you lose it? Indeed, you can lose a future only if you now in some sense have one. But how can you have something that does not yet exist? This shows, at the very least, that the ideas of having and losing in this context have very different meanings from when they occur in other, more usual contexts. It may be possible to have a future, but not in the same sense in which you might have broad shoulders or a Rolex watch. And if a murderer were to deprive you of your future, the sense of deprivation involved would be quite different from when age deprives you of your shoulders or a mugger deprives you of your watch.

If death is a bad thing for each one of us because it deprives us of a future, then a future must be something we have now, in the present time. We have a future because we have – actually and now – states that direct or bind us towards a future. These states are desires, goals and projects. Each one of us is, as Martin Heidegger put it, being-towards-a-future. Each one of us is, in our essential nature, directed towards a future that does not yet exist. And, in this sense at least, we can be said to have a future.

Let's begin with desires. The most basic feature of desires is that they can be satisfied or thwarted. Brenin's desire for a drink will be satisfied if he walks across the room to his bowl and drinks. It will be thwarted if he gets there and finds the bowl empty. However, satisfying a desire takes time. It also, typically, takes time for a desire to be thwarted. It takes time for Brenin to cross the room to his bowl; and so it takes time for his desire to be either satisfied or thwarted. This is one sense, the most basic sense, in which desires are future-directed: satisfying them takes time. The same is even more obviously true for goals and projects, both of which are essentially long-term desires. Desires can be satisfied or thwarted, and goals and projects can be fulfilled or unfulfilled. And satisfying and fulfilling take time.

However, there is a more complicated sense in which we can have a future. A desire, goal or project can be directed towards a future in two quite different ways. Like Brenin's desire for a drink of water, the desire can direct us towards a future in the sense that satisfying it takes time. If Brenin is to satisfy the desire, he must persist beyond the present moment – he must survive at least as long as it takes him to cross the room to his bowl. However, for some desires the connection with the future is stronger and more intimate than this. Some desires involve an explicit concept of the future. Walking across the room to drink something is one thing. Planning your life around a vision of how you would like your future to be is quite another.

Relative to other animals, we humans spend a disproportionate amount of time doing things that, at least on some level, we would really rather not do. We do this because of a vision of how we would like our future lives to be. This is the entire point of the slog through our prolonged education and subsequent careers. We all know how thankless the latter can be; and even I, a professional educator, can't pretend that the former is a non-stop barrel of laughs. But we do these things anyway because we have desires of a certain sort. These are desires that cannot be satisfied either now or in the immediate future but might, if we are talented enough, lucky enough and work hard enough, be satisfied at some unspecified future time. Our current activities – educational, vocational and often avocational – are devised and implemented with, and oriented towards, a vision of the future they may secure for us. To have these sorts of desires, you need to have a concept of the future: you must be able to think about the future as the future.

So, it seems, we can have a future in two different senses. There is an implicit sense: I have desires whose satisfaction takes time. And there is an explicit sense: I am orienting or arranging my life around a vision of how I would like the future to be. However, when the ape in us sees a distinction, it also sees a potential advantage. First, the ape identifies which of the distinguishable elements is most true of, or applies most naturally to, it. Then it claims that this element is superior to the other one. Believe me, I know: I am that ape.

It is the second sense of having a future that seems distinctive of human beings. It is not clear that other animals spend much, if any, of their time orienting their behaviour around a conception of how they would like their future to be. Delayed gratification seems to be a character trait that, while not unique to humans, is certainly more pronounced in humans than any other animal. And then the ape in us slides naturally from this factual claim to a moral evaluation based on it. The second sense of having a future, we inevitably think, is superior to the first. Of course, we are clever animals and we can back this moral evaluation up. In the second sense – where I organize myself and my life around a vision of how I would like the future to be – I am more closely tied to the future. I have my future in a stronger, more robust, more important sense than any other non-human animal does. Imagine two athletes, one dedicated and hard-working, the other a talented slacker. Both miss out on Olympic glory, finishing, let us suppose, just outside the medals. The first athlete, whose life has been formed and fashioned through iron discipline and faultless application, seems to lose more than the second athlete, who never really gave it their best shot. The first athlete's loss was greater because their investment – the time, effort, energy and emotion they put into what they were doing – was greater. What you lose when you die is a function of the investment you have made in that life. And because humans have a concept of the future, and so can discipline, organize and orient their present behaviour around a conception of how they would like their future to be, they make a greater investment in their lives than other animals. Therefore humans lose more when they die than other animals. Dying is worse for a human than for any other animal. Conversely, the life of a human is more important than that of any other animal. This is just one more facet of human superiority: we lose more when we die.

5

I used to believe this story. In fact, the last two sections were developed by yours truly – ape that I am – in *Animals Like Us* and also, somewhat more breezily, in *The Philosopher at the End of the Universe*. Now I cringe at my lack of insight and my ugly simian prejudices. Investment: how simian can you get? The fatal flaw, I now see, is not with the account itself. I think we humans are constrained to think of death as a harm of deprivation: that is, we are constrained to think that death is a bad thing because it takes something away from us. I don't think we're necessarily right to think of things in this way, but I don't think we are capable of thinking of it in any other way. Of course, some of us believe death is not the end – just a transition to a new form of existence, an afterlife. Who knows? They may be right. But I am not concerned with this issue. I'm concerned with whether the end of us is a bad thing – for the person whose end it is. And it doesn't matter how or when that end takes place. If you believe in any afterlife, then you probably believe in souls and God. And God, since He is omnipotent, can destroy souls. If God were to do that to you, it would, presumably, be the end of you. If so, would that be a bad thing – a bad thing for you? That is the question in which I am interested. It is the relation between us and our ends that is crucial – whatever forms those ends take.

Suppose the story I have told is true: humans do lose more when they die – or when they meet their end, whatever it is – than other animals. Death is a greater tragedy when it happens to a human than when it happens to a wolf. The mistake is to think that it follows from this that human lives are superior. That we lose more when we die is not an indication of our superiority; on the contrary, it is a clue to our damnation. The reason is that embodied in this account of death is a certain conception of time. And embodied in this conception of time is a vision of life's meaning.

The conception of time underlying the account of death I

have presented is a familiar one: time's arrow. The future is something we actually – and not merely possibly – have now, at the present time (whatever that means). And we have a future because we actually have – now – states that direct us towards that future: desires, goals, projects. Imagine these as arrows streaking into the future. Some of these arrows direct us into the future only implicitly: it takes time for them to reach their mark. To satisfy a desire, you have to survive long enough for the arrow of that desire to reach its mark. The desires of wolves and dogs are like this. However, some arrows are different. Some arrows are burning ones streaking out into the dark night of the future, and lighting up that future for us. Corresponding to these arrows are human desires, goals and projects that direct us towards the future explicitly by way of an overt conception of how that future is to be. Death harms any creature by cutting off the arrow of its desires in their flight. But death harms most those creatures whose arrows are burning ones.

It is by way of these sorts of metaphors that we humans try to understand time. We think of time as an arrow whose flight carries it from the past, through the present, into the future. Alternatively, we might think of time as a river flowing from the past to the future. Or we might think of it as a ship sailing from the past, passing through the present and heading into a distant and unknown future. We are caught up in this flow of time because we are temporal beings. Like other animals, the arrows of our desires pull us into, and allow us to hook on to, this temporal stream. And unlike other animals, our arrows can, to some extent, light up this stream – making it something to be seen, understood and perhaps shaped.

These are, of course, all metaphors. They are only

metaphors. What's more, they are all spatial metaphors. As Kant, among many others, noticed, whenever we try to understand time, we always seem to be pushed back to an analogy with space. More than that, however, these metaphors bring with them a certain conception of what is important in life: a certain conception of life's meaning.

The metaphors suggest a view of life's meaning as something towards which we must aim; or as a direction in which we must travel. The present is forever slipping away – the arrow of time constantly passing through one location on its way to the next. So, if the meaning of life is tied to moments, that meaning is also constantly slipping away. The meaning of our life, we think, must be tied to – must be a function of – our desires, goals and projects. The meaning of life is something towards which we can progress; something to be achieved. And as with all important achievements, this is not something that can happen now but only further on down the line.

However, we also know that further on down the line is to be found not meaning but its absence. If we follow the line far enough, we find not meaning but death and decay. We come to the point where all our arrows are cut off in their flight. We find the end of meaning. We are, each one of us, being-towards-a-future; and in this is to be found the possibility of our life having meaning. But we are also being-towards-death. The arrow of time is both our salvation and our damnation, and so we find ourselves both drawn to and repelled by this arrow's path. We are meaning-giving creatures – our lives have a meaning that, we think, the lives of other animals cannot have. We are death-bound beings, the beings who track death in a way that, we think, no other animal can. Both the meaning of our lives and the end of our lives are to be found somewhere further on down the line. The line, therefore, both fascinates us and horrifies us. This, fundamentally, is the existential predicament of human beings.

6

Quoth Edgar Allan Poe's raven: nevermore. Perhaps nevermore is a concept possessed by ravens. It is not, I suspect, one possessed by dogs. Nina loved Brenin. She grew up with him from the time she was a puppy. And she wanted to spend every waking second with him. True, by the time we got to France, perhaps even London, Brenin was nowhere near as interesting to her as Tess. Nina's interest in other dogs, or wolves, was a function of how much they would wrestle with her. And, by France, Brenin didn't really enjoy the rough and tumble any more. Nonetheless, she was always very affectionate towards him, greeting him with a big lick on the nose whenever she hadn't seen him for more than an hour or so.

So I was somewhat surprised when I brought Brenin's body back from the vet. Nina gave him a perfunctory sniff and then turned her attention to the apparently far more interesting business of playing with Tess. Brenin wasn't there any more: I'm pretty sure Nina understood that. I'm also pretty sure she couldn't grasp that Brenin would be there again nevermore.

We humans tend to suppose that this is evidence of a fundamental inferiority in animal intelligence. Animals cannot comprehend death; only humans can do that. Therefore we are better than they are. Once, I bought this. Now I suspect the inference goes the other way.

Suppose I were to take you to the same beach every day for a year, following the same path and doing the same things. After that I take you each day to the same *boulangerie*, where I buy you a *pain au chocolat* – not a *beignet framboise*, not a *croissant* but a *pain au chocolat*. Pretty soon, I am sure, you would be telling me: what, another *pain au chocolat*! Couldn't you have got me something else? Just for once? I'm sick of bloody *pains au chocolat*!

That is how it is with us humans. We think of the time of our lives as a line; and we have a very ambivalent attitude towards that line. The arrows of our desires, and our goals and our projects, bind us to this line, and therein do we find the possibility of our lives having meaning. But the line also points to the death that will take this meaning away. And so we are simultaneously attracted to and disgusted by this line, both drawn to and terrified of it. It is our fear of the line that makes us always want what is different. When our jaws close on the *pain au chocolat*, we can't help but see all the other *pains au chocolat* dotted out along the line, forwards and backwards. We can never enjoy the moment for what it is in itself because for us the moment is never what it is in itself. The moment is endlessly deferred both forwards and backwards. What counts as now for us is constituted by our memories of what has gone before and our expectations of things yet to come. And this is equivalent to saying that for us there is no now. The moment of the present is deferred, distributed through time: the moment is unreal. The moment always escapes us. And so for us the meaning of life can never lie in the moment.

Of course, we love our routines and rituals, some of us. But we also crave what is different. You should have seen the looks on the faces of my three canines when I started dividing up the *pains au chocolat* each morning. The quivering anticipation, the rivers of saliva, the concentration so intense it almost bordered on the painful. As far as they were concerned, it could be *pains au chocolat* from here to eternity. For them, the moment their jaws closed on the *pain au chocolat* was complete in itself, unadulterated by any other possible moments spread out through time. It could be neither augmented nor diminished by what had gone before and what was yet to come. For us, no moment is ever complete in itself. Every moment is adulterated, tainted by what we remember has been and what we anticipate will be. In each moment of our lives, the arrow of time holds us green and dying. And this is why we think we are superior to all other animals.

Nietzsche once talked of eternal recurrence, or the eternal return of the same. There are two different – but mutually compatible – ways of interpreting Nietzsche. At the very least, Nietzsche flirted with one of those ways; and he wholeheartedly endorsed the other. We might call the first the metaphysical interpretation of the eternal return. In this context, the word 'metaphysical' means a description of how things really are. So to understand the eternal return as a metaphysical doctrine is to think that it describes something that is actually going to happen – or, for that matter, has already happened – an infinite number of times. If you think that the universe is made up of only a finite number of particles – atoms or sub-atomic particles – then these particles can enter into only a finite number of combinations. Nietzsche actually thought of the universe as composed of a finite number of quanta or packets of power; but since these were capable of combination and recombination, the essential point remains the same. If you also think that time is infinite, it follows that the same combinations of particles or power quanta must recur. In fact, they must recur over and over again. But you, and the world around you, and the events that have made up your life, are just, ultimately, combinations of particles. So, it seems, you, your world and your life must recur over and over again. If time is infinite, then you must recur eternally.

This way of thinking about eternal recurrence is questionable, relying on the assumptions that the universe is finite and time is infinite. If you deny this – if, for example, you think that time is created with the creation of the universe and dies with that same universe – then the argument will not work. Nietzsche flirted with this interpretation of the eternal return, but never explicitly endorsed it in his published work.

What he did endorse in his published work was what we might call the existential interpretation of the eternal return. On this interpretation, the idea of eternal recurrence provides us with a sort of existential test. In his book *The Joyful Wisdom*, Nietzsche describes the test like this:

> *The greatest weight* – What, if some day or night a
> demon were to steal after you into your loneliest
> loneliness and say to you: 'This life as you now live it
> and have lived it, you will have to live once more and
> innumerable times more; and there will be nothing
> new in it, but every pain and every joy and every
> thought and sigh and everything unutterably small or
> great in your life will have to return to you, all in the
> same succession and sequence – even this spider and
> this moonlight between the trees, and even this

209

moment and I myself. The eternal hourglass of existence is turned upside down again and again, and you with it, speck of dust!' Would you not throw yourself down and gnash your teeth and curse the demon who spoke thus? Or have you once experienced a tremendous moment when you would have answered him: 'You are a god and never have I heard anything more divine.' If this thought gained possession of you, it would change you as you are or perhaps crush you.

Here the eternal return is not presented as a description of the way the world is, but something you should ask yourself if you want to understand both how your life is going and what sort of person you are. First of all, as Nietzsche puts it, all joy wants eternity. If your life is going well, you will be far more inclined to embrace the idea that your life will be repeated over and over again. If your life is not going well, on the other hand, you will probably regard the idea with horror. That much is obvious rather than deep. What is less obvious, perhaps, is how you react to the information imparted by the demon.

Suppose someone were to ask you: with whom do you want to spend eternity? Coincidentally, that might have been the question on the lips of the Jehovah's Witnesses who made the mistake of knocking on the door at Knockduff many years ago. Brenin and Nina were with me in the back garden and charged around to the front door to see who was there. When I got around there I found one of the Witnesses with his face to the wall, crying, while Brenin and Nina sniffed him, concerned expressions on their faces. I never did get to find out what they were going to ask me that day – they quickly excused themselves. But we naturally understand the question, 'With whom do you want to spend eternity?' as a religious one. Eternity is the afterlife and this, for all intents and purposes, is just a continuation of the line of our lives beyond the demise of our physical bodies. What we sometimes overlook in this picture is the one person you are unable to avoid in this eternity: you. The question religion then offers us is: are you sure you are a person with whom you would want to spend eternity? And this is a good question.

Nietzsche, however, makes the question far more urgent. If eternity is a continuation of the line of our lives, then whatever existential progress you make in this life you can continue on into the next. If life is a soul-making journey – a soul-making theodicy – then this journey can continue after the demise of your body. But suppose this life is it. Suppose your life is not a line. Suppose time is a circle and your life will be repeated over and over again, eternally recurring in the manner described by Nietzsche's demon. You are still the person with whom you are going to have to spend eternity. But eternity is now a circle and not a line, and so you have no further opportunity to improve or perfect yourself. Whatever you do you must do now.

If you are strong, Nietzsche thought, you will do what you feel you must do now. If, as he put it, your life and spirit are in the ascendant, then you will want to make yourself now the sort of person with whom you would want to spend eternity. But if you are weak, if your spirit is in decline – if you are tired – you will take refuge in deferral: in the idea that you can always do what you have to do later, in the life that is yet to come. The eternal return, then, is a way of judging whether you are a spirit in the ascendant or a spirit in decline. This is what I mean by saying that it is an existential test.

However, there is one more thing that the idea of the eternal return does, and I think it is the most important: it undermines the conception of life's meaning that is implied by the conception of time as a line. When we think of time as a line, we naturally think of the meaning of life as something towards which we must aim – as something to be achieved further on down the line. Each moment is always slipping away and so the meaning of life cannot be found in the moment. More than that, the significance of each moment derives from its place on the line: its significance consists in how it relates to what has gone before, which still exists in the form of memory, and what is yet to come, which exists in the form of anticipation. Each moment always carries the taint of the ghosts of past and future. Therefore, no moment is complete in itself – the content and meaning of every moment is deferred and distributed along the line of time's arrow.

But if time is a circle rather than a line, if one's life is destined to repeat itself over and over again without end, then the meaning of life cannot consist in progression towards some decisive point on the line. There is no such point because there is no such line. Moments do not slip away – on the contrary, they reassert themselves over and over again without end. The significance of each moment does not derive from its place on a line – on how it relates what comes before it on the line to what comes after. It does not carry the taint of past and future ghosts. Each moment is what it is; each moment is complete and entire in itself.

Now the meaning of life is quite different. Instead of being found at some or other decisive point on the line, or decisive portion of the line, the meaning of life is found in moments: not all moments – to be sure – just some of them. The meaning of one's life can be scattered through that life, like grains of barley scattered across the fields of Knockduff at harvest time. The meaning of life can be found in its highest moments. Each of these moments is complete in itself and requires no further moments for its significance or justification.

One thing I learned from the last year of Brenin's life is that wolves, and dogs for that matter, pass Nietzsche's existential test in a way that humans rarely do. A human would have said, 'Not the same old walk again today. Couldn't we go somewhere different for a change? I'm sick of the beach. And don't get me another *pain au chocolat* – I feel like I'm turning into one!' And so on and so forth. Alternately fascinated and repelled by time's arrow, our repulsion causes us to seek happiness in what is new and different, in any deviation from time's arrow. But our fascination with the arrow means that any deviation from the arrow's line simply creates a new line, and our happiness now requires that we deviate from this line too. The human search for happiness is, accordingly, regressive and futile. And at the end of every line is only nevermore. Nevermore to feel the sun on your face. Nevermore to see the smile on the lips of the one you love, or the twinkling in their eyes. Our conception of our lives and the meaning of those lives is organized around a vision of loss. No wonder time's arrow horrifies as well as fascinates us. No wonder we try to find our happiness in the new and unusual – in any deviation, no matter how small, from the arrow's path. Our rebellion may be nothing more than a futile spasm, but it is certainly understandable. Our understanding of time is our damnation. Wittgenstein was wrong, subtly but decisively. Death is not the limit of my life. Always, I have carried my death with me.

The time of wolves, I suspect, is a circle, not a line. Each moment of their lives is complete in itself. And happiness, for them, is always found in the eternal return of the same. If time is a circle, there is no nevermore. And, accordingly, one's existence is not organized around the vision of life as a process of loss. The regularity and repetition in our lives, during Brenin's last year, afforded me a fleeting and indistinct glimpse of the eternal return of the same. Where there is no sense of nevermore, there is no sense of loss. For a wolf or dog, death really is the limit of a life. And for this reason death has no dominion over them. This, I would like to think, is what it is to be a wolf or a dog.

I understand now why Nina gave Brenin's body only a perfunctory sniff, even though she loved him perhaps more than anything in the world. Of all of us, Nina understood time best. Nina was the keeper of time – the zealous guardian of the eternal return of the same. Every day, she knew exactly when it was 6 a.m. and I should drag myself out of bed to start work. Every day, she knew to the second when it was 10 a.m., and she would put her head in my lap to tell me that it was time to stop writing; that it was time to go to the beach. She knew when it was time to leave the beach to get to the *boulangerie* before it closed for lunch. Every day – whether it was standard or summer time, she knew exactly when it was 7 p.m. and their dinner should be presented, and then when it was time to walk to La Réunion for dessert. It was Nina's lifelong mission to preserve and guarantee the eternal return of the same. For her nothing could change; nothing could be different. She understood that real happiness lies only in what is the same, what is unchanging; what is eternal and immutable. Nina understood that it is the structure that is real, not the contingencies. She understood that all joy wants eternity; that if you have said yes to one moment you have said yes to them all. Her life was testament to the irrelevance of nevermore.

9

The Religion of the Wolf

1

We see through moments and for that reason the moment
escapes us. A wolf sees the moment but cannot see through
it. Time's arrow escapes him. That is the difference between
us and wolves. We relate to time in a different way. We are
temporal creatures in a way that wolves and dogs are not.
Indeed, according to Heidegger, temporality, as he called it, is
the essence of human beings. I am not concerned with the
question of what time really is. Neither, for that matter, was
Heidegger. No one knows what time really is – the excitable
pronouncements of some scientists notwithstanding – and I
suspect that no one ever will. It is the experience of time
that is crucial for us.

Actually, that is not quite right. It is my philosophical training that makes me look for sharp distinctions where there are
none. Philosophy is an act of power – some would say

hubris – where we try to impose our distinctions and divisions on a world that doesn't really accept them and isn't really suited to them. The world is too slippery for us. Instead of the divisions we would like to find, there are, I suspect, merely degrees of similarity and difference. A wolf is a creature of time as well as of the moment. It is just that we are more creatures of time, and less creatures of the moment, than is he. We are better at looking through moments than the wolf. And he is better at looking at moments than are we. The wolf is close enough to us for us to understand both what we gain by this and what we lose by it. If a wolf could speak, we could, I think, understand him.

The ape in us is quick to turn any difference to its advantage: any descriptive difference becomes immediately transformed into an evaluative one. The ape tells us that we are better than the wolf because we are more adept at looking through the moment. This conveniently forgets that the wolf is better at looking at the moment. If living with Brenin taught me one thing, it is that superiority is always superiority in one or another respect. More than that, superiority in one respect is likely to show up as a deficiency elsewhere.

Temporality – experiencing time as a line stretching from the past into the future – brings with it certain advantages, but also certain disadvantages. There are apes aplenty willing to extol the advantages of temporality. The purpose of this particular ape is to draw attention to the disadvantage: we cannot understand the significance of our own lives and, for precisely that reason, we find it so difficult to be happy.

During the last few weeks of Brenin's life, we did something together that illuminated for me just what it is to be a creature of the moment rather than a creature of time – a creature that is better suited to looking at moments than look-ing through them. By this time, I knew Brenin was going to die – at least I knew this intellectually, even if I was stead-fastly refusing to engage with it emotionally. I decided that Brenin needed a few days' break from Nina and Tess. They were always pestering him, even when he was trying to sleep – which, during his last days, was most of the time. It wasn't their fault. I couldn't take them for a walk, because that would have meant leaving Brenin by himself. And I didn't have the heart for that. I could imagine him wearily but determinedly struggling to his feet, spurred on by Nina and Tess's boisterous excitement, and being desperately unhappy when I told him he couldn't come with us. And I wasn't going to make him spend his last days like that. So, during the last few weeks, Nina and Tess had been restricted to the garden and house, and, understandably, they were becoming more and more hyper. I figured Brenin could do with a break, and so I took Nina and Tess to kennels in Issanka, a village about an hour or so up the road, in the direction of Montpellier. I decided I would leave them there just for a few days, to allow Brenin to get some quality rest.

When Brenin and I returned to the house – he had insisted on going with us to Issanka, of course – he gradually under-went a strange transformation. Indeed, quality rest seemed to be the last thing on his mind. He followed me around the house, bouncing up and down, yipping excitedly. When I made myself a plate of spaghetti, he demanded his share of it – something he hadn't done in a long, long time. So I asked him, 'Do you want to go for a walk?' His reaction, not quite the Buffalo Boy of old, but still quite impressive – he jumped up on to the sofa and howled – confirmed that he did indeed. I imagined us taking a gentle stroll over to the *digue* and walking along there for a few hundred yards or so. But when I got to the gate, Brenin was bounding around, running up and down the ditch that separated us from the nature reserve. So I did something I still can't quite believe even today.

I hadn't been running since shortly after we moved to France – and that was over a year ago. I tried, when we first arrived here, but I noticed that, after the first couple of miles, Brenin began to lag a long way behind us, and he wasn't happy about it at all. He had become old without me realizing it. So I replaced the runs with walks, punctuated with swimming on the beach and trips to the *boulangerie* and La Réunion. Nor had I been doing any other form of exercise. When I arrived I bought a set of weights and a bench. But it was only rarely I could talk myself into actually using them, and for the most part they sat, forlorn, on the sun terrace – a gently rusting reminder of how I had let myself go.

As Brenin had become older and weaker, I had become older and weaker too. That is often how it goes when you live with dogs. I had spent most of the year in France in a sort of premature retirement, doing some writing, but spending an awful lot of time soaking my feet in young wine. Nina and Tess, of course, were still up for long runs. But Brenin was not and we went for walks instead. And so, because of the peculiar way in which the composition of our lives had become entwined, Brenin's physical decline was mirrored by my own. Now I stood outside the house, and looked at Brenin running up and down the ditch, and said, 'Let's give it a go, my son. One last hurrah for the Rowlands boys. How about it?' So I dug out my shorts and we went running. I was watching Brenin carefully, and was fully expecting him to start tiring quickly. If so, I would have come straight home. But he didn't tire. We must have made quite a picture, the two of us: a dying wolf and a hopelessly out of shape man staring down the barrel of forty. We ran through the woods up to the Canal du Midi, ran along there in the shade of the giant beech trees that line its banks. Brenin ran alongside me, easily matching my stride. Then we cut through the nature reserve – following the fields of black bulls and white ponies of the ranches down to the *digue*. Still he didn't tire. Like the Brenin of old, he ghosted effortlessly over the ground, as if he were floating an inch or two above it, with me, his plodding, puffing, graceless ape, bumbling and stumbling along beside him.

Who knows? Perhaps he just wanted me on my own for a while. Perhaps he wanted to say goodbye, and couldn't do it properly with Nina and Tess dogging his steps. Whatever the reason, that day saw a distinct upturn in his energy and demeanour. And he never really lost it – not even the return of Nina and Tess in a few days' time could diminish it. We never went running together again – he never quite matched the energy levels of that day. But we went for a walk most days. He was OK. And he was OK almost until the day he died.

I can't help contrasting Brenin with how I would have been if I had cancer. For Brenin, cancer was an affliction of the moment. One moment he would feel fine. But another moment, an hour later, he would feel ill. But each moment was complete in itself and bore no relation to any other moment. For me, cancer would be an affliction of time, not an affliction of the moment. The horror of cancer – of any serious human illness – is the fact that it is spread out through time. Its horror lies in the fact that it will cut off the arrows of our desires, and our goals and projects: and we know it. I would have stayed at home to rest. I would have stayed home to rest even if I, at that moment, felt great. That is what you do when you have cancer. Because we are temporal creatures, our serious afflictions are temporal blights. Their horror consists in what they do through time, not in what they do at any moment. Because of this, they have a dominion over us that they cannot have over a creature of the moment.

The wolf takes each moment on its merits. And that is what we apes find so hard to do. For us, each moment is endlessly deferred. Each moment has a significance that depends on its relation to other moments and a content that is irredeemably tainted by those other moments. We are creatures of time, but wolves are creatures of the moment. Moments, for us, are transparent. They are what we reach through when we try to take possession of things. They are diaphanous. For us, moments are never fully real. They are not there. Moments are the ghosts of past and future, the echoes and anticipations of what was and what might be.

In his classic analysis of our experience of time, Edmund Husserl argued that the experience of what we call 'now' can be broken down into three different experiential components. There is, in part, an experience of what he called the primal now. But in our ordinary consciousness of time, this experience of the primal now is indelibly shaped by both anticipations of the likely future course of experience and recollections of its recent past. The former he called experiential protentions, the latter retentions. To see what he means, pick up something that lies to hand. You hold, let's suppose, a glass of wine in your hand. You experience it as a glass, presumably. But your fingers are not touching the entire glass, just parts of it. Even so, it feels to you as if you have a glass in your hand, not that you have parts of a glass in

your hand. Your experience of holding the glass is not constrained by the limits of your hands that allow you to have
this experience. Why? According to Husserl, it is because
your experience of holding the glass – an experience of something you are doing now – is made up of anticipations of
how your experience will change in given circumstances and
recollections of how it has changed in the recent past. For
example, you anticipate that if you slide your fingers down-
wards, you will encounter a narrowing of the field of your
touch, consistent with your holding the stem of the glass
rather than the bulb. Similarly, you might remember that
when you slid your fingers down the glass moments earlier,
your experience changed in this sort of way. Even an experience of the now, Husserl argued, is inextricably bound up
with experiences of the past and future.

This much, I am fairly sure, is true of wolves as well as
humans. We never experience the now as such – the primal
now is an abstraction, and does not correspond to anything
we can ever encounter in experience. What we call the now
is in part past and in part future. But differences of degree
can be just as important as differences of kind. We humans
have taken this to an entirely new level. So much of our
lives is spent living in the past or living in the future. Maybe,
when we try hard enough, we can experience the now in
something like the way a wolf does, as something only min-
imally written upon by retentions of the past and
protentions of the future. But this is not our ordinary way of
encountering the world. In us, and in our ordinary experience of the world, the now has been effaced: it has shrivelled
away to nothing.

There are many disadvantages of being a temporal creature; some obvious, some less so. An obvious one is that we

spend a large, perhaps disproportionate, amount of our time dwelling on a past that is no more and a future that is yet to be. Our remembered past and our desired future decisively shape what we laughably refer to as the here and now. Temporal creatures can be neurotic in a way that creatures of the moment cannot.

Temporality, however, also has drawbacks that are both more subtle and more important. There is a kind of temporal blight to which only humans are subject because only humans live enough in the past and future for this affliction to take hold. Because we are better at looking through moments than looking at them – because we are temporal animals – we both want our lives to have meaning and are unable to understand how our lives could have meaning. Temporality's gift to us is the desire for what we cannot understand.

2

Sisyphus was a mortal who had offended the gods in some way. In precisely what way is not really known and stories differ. Perhaps the most popular account is that after his death, Sisyphus talked Hades into allowing him to return temporarily to earth, on an urgent mission of some sort, and promised to return as soon as his mission was complete. However, when he had again seen the light of day and felt the warmth of the sun on his face, Sisyphus had no wish to return to the dark of the underworld. And so he didn't. Ignoring numerous admonitions and disregarding explicit instructions to return, Sisyphus managed to live many more years in the light. Eventually, following a decree of the gods, he was forcibly returned to the underworld; and there was made ready his rock.

Sisyphus's punishment was to roll a huge rock up a hill. When this task was completed, after many days, weeks or even months of exhausting labour, the rock would roll back down the hill, to the very bottom, and Sisyphus would have to begin his labour all over again. And that was it, for all eternity. This is a truly horrible punishment, embodying a cruelty of which perhaps only the gods would be capable. But in what, exactly, does its horror lie?

The way the myth is usually told emphasizes the difficulty of Sisyphus's labour. The rock is typically described as massive, of a size he is barely capable of moving. Thus Sisyphus's every step up the hill taxes his heart and nerves and sinews to their limits. But, as Richard Taylor has pointed out, it is doubtful that the true horror of Sisyphus's punishment lies in its difficulty. Suppose the gods had given him, instead of a massive boulder, a small pebble – one that he might easily fit in his pocket. Sisyphus, then, might take a leisurely stroll to the top of the hill. Watch the pebble roll down and begin his labour all over again. Despite the less arduous nature of this task, the horror of Sisyphus's punishment is, I think, scarcely mitigated.

We are the animals that think what is most important in life is happiness. Because of this, we are strongly tempted to suppose that the horror of Sisyphus's punishment lies in the fact that he hates it – the punishment makes him so unhappy. But I don't think this is correct either. We can only assume that Sisyphus reviles his fate. However, suppose the gods were less vengeful than they are represented in the myth. Suppose they, in fact, took steps to mitigate his unhappiness; steps that were aimed at reconciling Sisyphus with his destiny. They did this by implanting in Sisyphus an irrational, but nevertheless intense, compulsion to roll rocks up hills. We needn't worry too much about how they did this; it is the result that is important. And the result is that Sisyphus is now never happier than when he is rolling rocks up hills. In fact, if he is not allowed to roll rocks uphill, he becomes distinctly frustrated, even depressed. And so the mercy of the gods takes the form of making Sisyphus desire, indeed embrace with all his heart, the very punishment they have inflicted on him. His one true desire in life is to roll rocks up hills, and he is guaranteed its eternal fulfilment. This mercy of the gods is no doubt perverse; but it is nonetheless mercy.

Indeed, it is mercy so complete that perhaps there is no real sense in which Sisyphus's task can any longer be regarded as a punishment. If anything, it seems more reward than punishment. If happiness is feeling good about life, feeling that life and everything in it is wonderful, Sisyphus's new existential situation seems optimal. No one could be happier than Sisyphus, guaranteed the eternal fulfilment of his deepest desire. If happiness is what is most important in life, then it should be impossible to imagine a better life than that of Sisyphus.

However, it seems to me that the horror of Sisyphus's punishment is not diminished one iota by the mercy of the gods. Sometimes the rewards of the gods can be worse than their retributions. I think we should now feel even sorrier for Sisyphus than we did before. Prior to the 'mercy' of the gods, Sisyphus at least possessed some sort of dignity. Powerful but vicious beings have imposed his fate on him. He recognizes the futility of his labour. He performs this labour through necessity. There is nothing else he can do – not even die. But he recognizes the futility of his task and he has contempt for the gods who have imposed it on him. This dignity is lost once the gods become merciful. Now our contempt, tinged with sympathy perhaps but contempt nonetheless, must be directed as much at Sisyphus as at the gods who made him that way: Sisyphus the dupe, Sisyphus the deluded, Sisyphus the stupid. Perhaps on those long trudges back down the hill, Sisyphus sometimes dimly recalls the times before the mercy of the gods. Perhaps some small, still voice in the backwaters of his soul calls out to him. And perhaps then, briefly, Sisyphus understands, through echoes and whispers, what has happened to him. And he realizes that he has become a diminished thing. Sisyphus understands that he has lost something important; more important than the happiness he now enjoys. The mercy of the gods has taken from Sisyphus the possibility that his life – or rather his after-life – will amount to anything more than a sick joke. It is precisely this possibility that is more important than his happiness.

I doubt that we are the sorts of animals that can be happy, a least not in the way we think of happiness. Calculation – our simian schemes and deceptions – has permeated too deeply into our souls for us to be happy. We chase the feelings that come with the success of our machinations and mendacities, and we shun the feelings that come with their failure. No sooner have we taken one mark than we are looking for the next. We are always on the make and our happiness, consequently, slips through our grasp. Feeling – and this is what we take happiness to be – is a creature of the moment. For us, there is no moment – every moment is endlessly deferred. Therefore for us there can be no happiness.

But at least we can understand now our obsession with feelings: this is a symptom of something far deeper. Our preoccupation with feeling a certain way – the widespread assumption that this is what is most important in life – is an attempt to reclaim something that our living in the past and in the future has taken from us: the moment. This, for us, is no longer a real possibility. But even if we could be happy – even if we were the sorts of creatures for which happiness is a real possibility – that is not what it is about.

3

The real horror of Sisyphus's punishment, of course, lies neither in its difficulty nor in the fact that it makes Sisyphus so desperately unhappy. The horror of the punishment lies in its sheer futility. It is not simply that Sisyphus's task comes to nothing. You can be faced with a meaningful task that you fail to achieve. Your efforts, then, come to nothing. This may be a source of sadness and regret. But there is no horror. The horror of Sisyphus's task, whether it is easy or difficult, whether he loves it or detests it, lies not in the fact that he fails but in that there is nothing that would count as success. Whether he gets the boulder to the top or not, it still rolls down and he must begin again. His labour is futile. It aims at nothing. His task is as barren as the boulder.

This might tempt us into thinking that if only we could find a purpose for Sisyphus's task, then everything would be all right. It would be purpose, rather than happiness, that is the most important thing to find in life – whether the life is that of Sisyphus or anyone else. But, once again, I don't think this can be correct. To see why, suppose there was a point to Sisyphus's labour. Suppose there was a goal towards which his efforts aimed. Instead of the boulder rolling back down the hill, it stayed put at the top. And his trudges back down the hill were therefore not to collect the same boulder, but different ones. The command of the gods was now to build a temple, one that was mighty and beautiful, a fitting tribute, as they saw it, to their own power and magnificence. Suppose also, if you like, that, being merciful gods, they inculcated an intense desire in Sisyphus to do just this. After ages of grim and dreadful toil, we might imagine him succeeding in his task. The temple is now complete. He can rest on that high mountain and regard with satisfaction the fruits of his labour. There's just one question: what now?

There is the rub. If you think of what is most important in life as a goal or purpose, then as soon as that purpose is achieved your life no longer has meaning. Just as Sisyphus's existence in the original telling of the tale has no meaning because it has no purpose, so too, in our retelling, Sisyphus's existence loses whatever meaning it has as soon as his purpose is complete. His life on that high mountain, gazing for ever at a goal he can neither change nor add to, is as meaningless as his life rolling a huge and intransigent boulder up a hill only to see it roll down again as soon as he reaches the summit.

We think of time as a line stretching from the past into the future, with the lives of each one of us laid out as overlapping segments of this line. Perhaps this is why it is so natural for us to think of what is important in life as a goal towards which our lives are directed – as something towards which we are progressing. What is most important in life is something we have to work towards. It is a function of our life's goals and projects. And if we work hard enough, and are talented enough, and, perhaps, are lucky enough, this is something we can achieve. It is not, of course, exactly clear when this may happen. Some think that what is most important in life can be achieved in this life. Many think that it can be achieved only in the next life, and that the importance of this life is simply a matter of preparing us for the next. But even casual reflection on the case of Sisyphus should convince us that the meaning of life cannot be like this. Whatever else the meaning of life is, it cannot consist in progression towards some goal or end point – whether the point is in this life or the next.

The myth of Sisyphus is, of course, an allegory for human life (and indeed was used as such by the French existentialist philosopher Albert Camus). The allegory is not subtle. The life of each and every one of us is like one of Sisyphus's journeys to the summit, and each day in our life is as one of Sisyphus's steps on this journey. The only difference is this: Sisyphus himself returns to push the bolder up the hill once more, while we leave this to our children.

As you go to work today, or school or wherever it is you go, look at the bustling throng. What are they doing? Where are they going? Focus on one of them. Perhaps he is going to an office where he will do the same things today as he did yesterday, and where he will do the same things tomorrow as he does today. On the inside, he may pulsate with energy and purpose. The report has to be on the desk of Ms X by 3 p.m. – this is crucial – and he must not forget the meeting with Mr Y at 4.30 p.m. – and if this does not go well the consequences for performance in the North American market will be grim. He understands all of these as very important things. Perhaps he enjoys these things, perhaps not. He does them anyway because he has a home and a family and must raise his children. Why? So that in a few years' time they can do much the same things as him for much the same reasons, and produce children of their own, who, in turn, do much the same things for much the same reasons. They will then be the ones worrying about reports and meetings and performance in the North American market.

This is the existential dilemma revealed to us by Sisyphus. Like the man who must meet Ms X and Mr Y, and worry about the North American market, we can fill our lives with little goals, diminutive purposes. But these cannot provide our life with meaning, because these goals aim only at their own repetition – either by us or by our children. But if we were to find a purpose that was somehow grand enough to give meaning to our lives – and I'm not sure I have any idea what such a purpose would be – then we must, at all costs, make sure we don't achieve this purpose. As soon as we do, our life would once again lack meaning. It would be nice, of course, if we could time the achieving of our grand meaning-giving purpose to coincide with our last, dying, breath. But what sort of purpose can be achieved when we are at our weakest? And if we can achieve it when we are at our weakest, why could we not have done so before? Are we to think of the meaning of life as being like a fish we have had on a hook for some time and are simply waiting until we die to pull it out? What sort of meaning is that? And how much of a fish can it really be if we are able to pull it out of the water as the strength slips from us?

If we assume that the meaning of life consists in a purpose, then we must hope we never achieve that purpose. If the meaning of life consists in a purpose, a necessary condition of life continuing to have meaning is our failure to achieve that purpose. As far as I can see, this is to make the meaning of life into a hope that can never be fulfilled. But what is the point of a hope that can never be fulfilled? A futile hope cannot give life meaning. Sisyphus no doubt entertained the futile hope that the boulder would, for the first time ever, stay at the top of the hill where he left it. But this hope did not give Sisyphus's life meaning. The meaning of life, I think we should conclude, is not to be found in a progression towards an end point or goal. There is no meaning in the end.

4

If the meaning of life is not happiness and it is not purpose, then what is it? Indeed, what sort of thing could it possibly be? In connection with philosophical problems, Wittgenstein used to speak of the decisive movement in the conjuring trick. A seemingly insoluble philosophical problem, Wittgenstein thought, will always turn out to be based on one or another assumption that we have unconsciously, and ultimately illicitly, smuggled into the debate. This assumption decisively sets us on a certain way of thinking about the problem. And the impasse we eventually, but inevitably, reach is an expression not of the problem itself but of the assumption that has caused us to think about the problem in the way that we have.

For the meaning of life, here is my suggestion for the decisive movement in the conjuring trick. We have assumed that what is most important in life is to have something. If our lives are a line constituted by the arcing arrows of our desires, then we can possess whatever those arrows encompass. In the nineteenth-century American West, settlers were sometimes promised as much land as they could cover in a day's ride. This was called a land grab. We think that we can, in principle, possess whatever the arrows of our desires, goals and projects can cover. Whatever is most important in life – the meaning of our lives – can, through talent, industry and perhaps luck, be grabbed. This might be happiness, or it might be a purpose. Both of these are things that one can have. But this, I learned from Brenin, is not how it is with the meaning of life. The most important thing in life – the meaning of life, if that is how you want to think of it – is to be found in precisely what we cannot have.

The idea that the meaning of life is something that can be possessed is, I suspect, a legacy of our grasping simian soul. For an ape, having is very important. An ape measures itself in terms of what it has. But for a wolf it is being rather than having that is crucial. For a wolf what is most important in life is not to possess a given thing or a quantity. It is to be a certain type of wolf. But even if we acknowledge this, our simian soul will soon try to reassert the primacy of possession. To be a certain type of ape – that is something towards which we can strive. To be a certain type of ape is simply one more purpose that we can have. The ape that we most want to be is something towards which we can progress. It is something to be achieved if we are sufficiently clever, sufficiently industrious and sufficiently lucky.

The most important and difficult lesson to learn in life is that this is not how things are. What is most important in life is not something that you can ever possess. The meaning of life is to be found precisely in those things that temporal creatures cannot possess: moments. This is why it is so difficult for us to identify a plausible meaning for our lives. Moments are the one thing that we apes cannot possess. Our possession of things is based on effacing the moment – moments are things we reach through in order to possess the objects of our desires. We want to possess the things we value, stake claim to those things; our lives are one big land grab. And because of this we are creatures of time, not creatures of the moment: the moment that always slips through our grasping fingers and opposable thumbs.

In saying that the meaning of life is to be found in moments, I am not repeating those facile little homilies that entreat us to 'live in the moment'. I would never recommend trying to do something that is impossible. Rather, the idea is that there are some moments, not all of them by any means, but there are some moments; and in the shadows of these moments we will find out what is most important in our lives. These are our highest moments.

5

The expression 'highest moments' will no doubt mislead us, pointing us back in the direction of the view of life's meaning we should reject. We are likely to think of our highest moments in one of three ways, all of which are erroneous. The first way is to think of our highest moments as ones towards which our life can progress – as moments towards which our lives are building, moments that can be achieved if we are sufficiently talented and industrious. But our highest moments are not the culmination of our lives – they are not the towards-which of our existence. The highest moments of our lives are scattered through those lives. These are moments scattered through time: the ripples made by a wolf as he splashes in the warm summer waters of the Mediterranean.

We are so conditioned to thinking of what is important in life as happiness, which we understand as feeling good, that all talk of highest moments will inevitably bring to mind some kind of nirvana-like state of intense pleasure. This is the second way of misunderstanding what I mean by highest moments. In fact, our highest moments are rarely pleasant ones. Sometimes they are the most unpleasant times imaginable – the darkest moments of our lives. Our highest moments are when we are at our best. And often it takes something truly horrible for us to be so.

There is another, more subtle and more insidious but equally erroneous way of thinking about higher moments. This is that our highest moments reveal to us what we really are. These are the moments, we think, that define us. There is a persistent trend in Western thought for thinking of the self or person as the sort of thing that can be defined. Echoing Shakespeare, we solemnly intone sayings like: *to thine own self be true*. This suggests that there is such a thing as a true you, and that you can either be true or false to this you. I seriously doubt if this is how things are. I seriously doubt if there is a true you, or me for that matter – a self or person that persists through and transcends all the different ways in which we might be false to it. In fact, I doubt this was even Shakespeare's view – putting it, as he did, in the mouth of a manifest fool like Polonius (and thanks to Colin McGinn for convincing me of this).

So, I doubt there is a real me, as opposed to a false me. There is just me. Indeed, I am no longer sure that there is even that. What I call me may just be a succession of different people, all psychologically and emotionally related, and all united by the illusion that they are all me. Who knows? It doesn't really matter. The crucial point is that each of my highest moments is complete in itself and does not require justification in the supposed role it plays in defining who and what I am. It is the moments that are important and not the person that they are (erroneously) supposed to reveal. That is the hard lesson.

I am a professional philosopher and therefore a stubborn form of scepticism is, or should be, my stock in trade. Poor old God, after all the trouble He took with me – the absurdly improbable intervention in the form of Brenin's stone ghost – and I still can't quite bring myself to believe in Him. But if I could believe, then I would hope God was the God of Eli Jenkins's prayer in *Under Milk Wood*: the God who would always look for our best side and not our worst. Our highest moments reveal our best side and not our worst. The me at my worst is as real as the me at my best. But what makes me worth it – if I am – is the me at my best.

I was at my best, I am convinced, when I was saying no to Brenin's death during those early days in France. I was a sleep-deprived deep shade of crazy. I thought I was dead and in hell. My view of what was going on in my life made Tertullian sound positively reasonable. I was sectionable. But, nonetheless, these were among the highest moments of my life. This is what Sisyphus eventually understood. We are at our best when there is no point in going on; when there is no hope for which to go on. But hope is a form of desire, and so it is what makes us temporal creatures – the arrows of our hope arcing off into the undiscovered country of our future. And sometimes it is necessary to put hope in its place – to put it back in its sleazy little box. And so we go on anyway – and in doing so we make a point (although that, of course, is not why we do it – any reason would undermine the point). In those moments, we say, 'F**k you!' to the gods of Olympus, to the gods of this world or the next, and their plans for us to roll rocks up hills for all eternity – either that or foist the job on our children. To be at our best we have to be pushed into a corner, where there is no hope and nothing to be gained from going on. And we go on anyway.

We are at our best when death is leaning over our shoulder and there is nothing we can do about it and our time is nearly done. But we say, 'F**k you!' to the line of our lives and embrace instead the moment. I am going to die, but in this moment I feel good and I feel strong. And I am going to do what I will. This moment is complete in itself and needs no further justification in other moments, past or future.

We are at our best when the ninety-five-pound pit bull of life has us by the throat and pinned to the ground. And we are just three-month-old cubs and can be easily torn apart. There is pain coming, and we know it, and there is no hope. But we don't whine or yelp. We don't even struggle. Instead, there emanates from deep inside of us a growl, a growl that is calm and sonorous, that belies our tender age and existential fragility. That growl says, 'F**k you!'

Why am I here? After four billion years of blind and unthinking development, the universe produced me. Was it worth it? I seriously doubt it. But I am here to say, 'F**k you!' anyway – when the gods have given me no hope, when Cerberus, the dog of the pit, has me pinned to the ground by the neck. It's not my happy moments; it is these moments, I now know, that are my highest moments, because they are my most important moments. And they are important because of what they are in themselves, not because of any supposed role they play in defining who I am. If I am, in any shape or form, worth it – if I am a worthwhile thing for the universe to have done – then it is these moments that make me so.

And so it was, I suppose, a wolf that revealed all this to

me; he was the light and I could see myself in the shadow he cast. What I learned was, in effect, the antithesis of religion. Religion always deals in hope. If you are a Christian or a Muslim, it is the hope that you will be worthy of heaven. If you are a Buddhist, it is the hope that you will attain release from the great wheel of life and death and so find nirvana. In the Judaeo-Christian religions, hope is even elevated into the primary virtue and renamed faith.

Hope is the used-car salesman of human existence: so friendly, so plausible. But you cannot rely on him. What is most important in your life is the you that remains when your hope runs out. Time will take everything from us in the end. Everything we have acquired through talent, industry and luck will be taken from us. Time takes our strength, our desires, our goals, our projects, our future, our happiness and even our hope. Anything we can have, anything we can possess, time will take it from us. But what time can never take from us is who we were in our best moments.

6

There is a painting called *Lone Wolf*, by Alfred von Kowalski. It depicts a wolf standing at night on a snow-capped hill, looking down at a small log cabin. The cabin has smoke rising from its chimney and a light glowing warmly in its window. The cabin always reminded me of Knockduff, when I returned from one of our winter evening walks, with Brenin and the girls trotting ahead of me, away from the darkness of the woods and towards the welcoming light I had left on in the window. Kowalski's picture is, of course, allegorical – a depiction of the outsider looking in on the warm and cosy comfort of someone else's life. But perhaps the cabin reminded me of Knockduff only because the wolf reminded me of me and the life I had lived.

One way or another, that life came to an end, or at least began to draw to its conclusion, on that dark January night in Languedoc when I put Brenin in the ground and raged against God and nearly drank myself to death. I sometimes wonder if I really died that night. Descartes, on his own long, dark night of the soul, found his refuge in a God who would not deceive him. Descartes could doubt almost everything – that there was a physical world around him, that he had a physical body. He could, gifted mathematician and logician that he was, doubt the truths of mathematics and logic. But he could not doubt that there existed a God who was kind and good. This God would not let him be deceived, as long as he took sufficient care in evaluating his beliefs.

I think Descartes was probably wrong about this. There is a difference between a good God and a kind God. A good God might not let us be deceived. But a kind God almost certainly would. The highest moments of our lives are so hard and so withering. There is a reason the worth of our lives can only be revealed to us in moments. We are not strong enough for it to be revealed in any other way. Although I am not a religious man in any conventional sense of that term, sometimes, when I remember the night of Brenin's death, when I looked across the flames of his funeral pyre and saw his stone ghost looking back at me, I think that God was telling me: *It's OK, Mark, it really is. It doesn't have to be hard all the time. You are safe.* This feeling, I think, is the essence of the religion of humans.

So I sometimes wonder if this is, perhaps, the astonish-ingly beautiful dream of a dead man, bequeathed him by a kind God, rather than the good God of Descartes. This is a God who would let me be deceived, precisely because that is what a kind God does. This was the same God I cursed with my dying breath.

I wonder this because if God had appeared to me that night, given me a pen and paper and asked me to write down how I wanted my life to be from now on, I couldn't have written it better. I'm now married – to Emma, not only the most beautiful woman I've ever seen, but the kindest person I've ever known: someone who is unquestionably, demonstrably, irredeemably and categorically superior to me.

My career has spiralled ever upwards – from a humble lecturer at an even humbler university, whom nobody wanted to know, I'm now offered improbably inflated salaries by top universities in the US. My books have become bestsellers – or, at least, what passes for bestsellers in the rarefied atmosphere of academic publishing. And I am no longer the sort of person who is capable, or who would even consider, drinking two litres of Jack in a single sitting, no matter what the circumstances or motivation. As you must have realized, you don't get to be the sort of person who can drink like that without many, many years of consistent and dedicated practice.

I'm not saying this to gloat, or because I am especially pleased with myself. Quite the contrary: I am genuinely – staggeringly – bemused. I say it because I know that none of it is, in the end, what makes me worth it. I would be lying if I said I wasn't proud. But, at the same time, I'm wary of this pride. This is the pride of the ape, of my sulking, skulking simian soul: the soul which thinks that what is most important in life is to guide oneself to the top of the pile through instrumental reason and all that goes with it. But when I remember Brenin, I remember also that what is most important is the you that remains when your calculations fail – when the schemes you have schemed shudder to a halt, and the lies you have lied stick in your throat. In the end, it's all luck – all of it – and the gods can take away your luck as quickly as they confer it. What is most important is the person you are when your luck runs out.

On that night I buried Brenin, in the rosy warmth of his funeral fire and the sharp and biting cold of the Languedoc night, we find the fundamental human condition. A life lived in the rosy warmth and kindness of hope is the one any of us would choose if we could. We would be mad not to. But what is most important when the time comes – and it always will – is to live your life with the coldness of a wolf. Such a life is too hard, too wintry, and we could only wither. But there come moments when we can live it. It is these moments that make us worth it because, in the end, it is only our defiance that redeems us. If wolves had a religion – if there was a religion of the wolf – that is what it would tell us.

7

I couldn't leave Brenin's bones lying all alone in the South of France. So I bought a house in the same village. On our daily walks, we would say hello to his stone ghost as we passed. However, I'm writing these concluding sentences from Miami. I succumbed, eventually, to one of the aforementioned improbably inflated salaries. Emma and I arrived here a few months ago. Nina and Tess are still around, and it goes without saying that they came with us. Nina still wakes me up each day at 6 a.m., and if my hands or feet are not exposed outside the bedsheet, she'll rearrange the sheet until they are. Lick, lick: don't you know we have people to see and places to go? But they're beginning to show their age. They spend most of their days sleeping – out by the pool, or in the garden, or on the sofa. I can't go running with them any more. That is something I returned to after Brenin's death – much to their delight. But now they fall behind me after the first mile or so and there's just no point. Perhaps I'll grow fat and slow for a while with my two girls, just as I did with Brenin. But they do enjoy their gentle walks along the Old Cutler Road, where they still find the energy to intimidate the American dogs they meet, which are all far too enthusiastic and excitable – too young – for Nina and Tess's predilections. I'm sure they're delighted that all the local dogs are terrified of them. They, and their owners, cross the street to avoid us. But that's OK. If I know Nina and Tess at all, I'm pretty sure they would want to go out as top dogs. But they're fading, the two of them. The warmth is really good for Nina's arthritis – and, believe me, I know how she feels.

Sometimes I get a feeling; it's the strangest feeling. It's that I used to be a wolf and I'm now just a stupid Labrador. Brenin has come to represent to me a part of my life that is no more. The feeling is bittersweet. I am sad because I am no longer the wolf that I was. And I'm happy because I'm no longer the wolf that I was. But above all I once was a wolf. I am a creature of time, but I still remember that it's the highest moments that count – moments scattered through your life like grains of barley at harvest time – not where you start and not where you end up. Perhaps one cannot remain a wolf all one's life. But that is never what it was about. One day the gods will once again decide to give me no hope. Perhaps this will be soon. I hope not; but it's going to happen. When it does, I shall do my best to remember the wolf cub pinned to the ground by his neck.

But here is the truth of the pack: our moments are never our own. Sometimes my memories of Brenin are tinged with a strange sort of amazement. It's as if the memories are made up of two partially overlapping images: one senses that the images are connected in an important way, but they're too blurred to make out. And then they suddenly converge – snap into focus – like images in an old kaleidoscope. I remember Brenin next to me, striding the touchlines of the rugby pitch in Tuscaloosa. I remember him sitting next to me at the post-match party, when pretty Alabama girls would come up and say, 'I just love your dog.' I remember him running with me through the streets of Tuscaloosa; and when the Tuscaloosa city streets transform into lanes of an Irish countryside, I remember the pack running next to me, easily matching its stride to mine. I remember the three of them bouncing like salmon through the seas of barley. I remember Brenin dying in my arms in the back of the Jeep as the vet inserts the needle into the vein on his front right leg. And when the convergence of images happens, I think: is that really me? Was it really me that did those things? Is that really my life?

This realization sometimes strikes me as a faintly surreal discovery. It is not me I remember striding the touchline in Tuscaloosa; it is the wolf that walked beside me. It is not me I remember at the party, it is the wolf that sat beside me and the pretty girls that approached me because of this. It is not me I remember running through the streets of Tuscaloosa or the country lanes of Kinsale; it is the wolves who matched their stride to mine. My memory of myself is always dis-placed. That I am in these memories at all is not given; sometimes it is a fortuitous bonus that must be discovered.

The Religion of the Wolf

I never remember myself. I remember myself only through my memories of others. Here we are decisively confronted with the fallacy of egoism; the fundamental error of the ape. What is important is not what we have but who we were when we were at our best. And who we were when we were at our best is only revealed to us in moments – our highest moments. But our moments are never our own. Even when we are truly alone, when the pit bull has us pinned to the ground, and we are but cubs and easily broken, it is the dog we remember and not ourselves. Our moments – our most wonderful and our most terrifying moments – these become ours only through our memories of others, whether these others are good or evil. Our moments belong to the pack, and we remember ourselves through them.

If I had been a wolf instead of an ape, then I would be referred to as a disperser. Sometimes a wolf will leave its pack and head off into the woods, never to return. They have begun a journey and they will never again go home. No one is sure why they do this. Some postulate a genetic longing to breed, coupled with an unwillingness to wait their turn to move up the pack's hierarchy. Some argue that dispersers are especially antisocial wolves who don't enjoy the company of other wolves in the way that normal wolves do. I can identify, in my way, with both accounts. But who knows? Perhaps some wolves just think there is a big old world out there and it would be a shame not to see as much of it as they can. In the end, it doesn't really matter. Some dispersers die alone. Others, the lucky ones, meet other dispersers and form packs of their own.

And so, by some strange twist of fate, my life is now the best it has ever been – at least if we judge that in terms of how happy I am. As I write these sentences, Emma is poised to go into labour. Well, I say 'poised' to go into labour, but she's been poised for a few days now. There are lots of pronounced uterine rumblings, but nothing organized or regular enough to be decisive. Nonetheless, I live in hope. I'm fully expecting to hear her call out at any moment for me to grab the bag and drive her to South Miami Hospital. So I must be brief. After forty years as a rootless and restless disperser, I have finally found a human pack. My first child, my son, will be born any day now – and I have a feeling, a sneaking suspicion that I can't quite shake, that it's going to be today. And I hope this doesn't give him too much to live up to, but I think I just might call him Brenin.

Brenin: I worry about your bones, lying 3,000 miles away in France. I hope you're not too lonely. I miss you, and I miss seeing your stone ghost every morning. But, the gods willing, our pack will be there again soon, for Languedoc's never-ending summer. Until then, sleep well, my wolf brother. We'll meet again in dreams.